Podolia
Neſter fl.
Prut fl.
Getę
Moldau
Cronſtat
Brayle
Ternis
Kilia
Pontus
Alt fl.
Bulgaria

TRANSYLVANIA

FRANCES LINCOLN LIMITED
PUBLISHERS

TRANSYLVANIA

Bronwen Riley
Photographs Dan Dinescu

FRANCES LINCOLN LIMITED
PUBLISHERS

To my friends in the Apuseni Mountains

Frances Lincoln
4 Torriano Mews
Torriano Avenue
London NW5 2RZ

www.franceslincoln.com

First published in 2007 by Frances Lincoln

Designed by **Georgina Rhodes**
Edited by **Nancy Marten**

British Library Cataloguing in Publication Data

A catalogue record of this book is available from the British Library

ISBN 978-0-7112-2781-1
Printed in Singapore

9 8 7 6 5 4 3 2 1

Note on personal and place names: *the current official Romanian place name, followed by its German or Hungarian name in brackets, is given on its first mention. For personal names, the first name has generally been anglicised and the surname given in its most common form.*

Contents

Left: *On All Souls' Day, at the beginning of November, a service is held in the cemetery to commemorate the dead.*
Previous page: *Horses, haystack and wooden church in a Maramureş landscape.*
Title page: *Sturdy Saxon houses in the medieval fortified town of Sighişoara (Schässburg).*

Left: *Wooden house in a high settlement in the Carpathians.*

Introduction

We are in Transylvania; and Transylvania is not England. Our ways are not your ways, and there shall be to you many strange things.
Bram Stoker, *Dracula*

When I was young, I dreamed of stepping back in time. I longed to find the magic wardrobe or secret passage that would spirit me to a distant age and show me how people lived before I was born. Years later, my wish was granted more easily than I could ever have imagined, when I boarded a night train in Budapest and woke up in Transylvania. As I looked out of the train window and saw the horses and carts plodding alongside, I knew that I had been transported into another time. Station-masters in smart uniforms stood to attention as the train passed their stations, almost as though the Austro-Hungarian Empire had never ended. Always looming in the background were the Carpathians, their jagged snow-covered peaks guarding Transylvania in a grand, sweeping crescent from unspeakable dangers further east.

Later on that first journey, lost in the forest, we were rescued by a woodcutter who gave us a ride in his horse-drawn cart. We lay on thick sheepskins, looking up at the moon through the snow-laden trees. On subsequent journeys, while helping with the haymaking in high pastures, hearing magic spells, or being welcomed by

people whose houses were lit by oil lamps and whose lives were governed by their religion and the seasons, I felt that I better understood life before the industrial age.

Transylvania is a land created for the romantic. It has all the elements of Romanticism – dramatic mountains and great forests, wild animals and ancient ruins, a rural landscape of great beauty with an assortment of picturesque individuals in traditional dress: gypsies, shepherds and the occasional hermit. Wood-cutters, witches, jolly millers, tragic orphans, bears and wolves live in the great forests and the towns and villages founded by Saxon settlers in the Middle Ages; it is a folk-tale come to life. Of course, not all fairy stories have happy endings. So, too, within a wildly romantic landscape are poverty, poor health and, never far away in the industrialised towns and cities, the ugly vestiges of a Communist past.

Many people believe that Transylvania is a fictitious country, like Ruritania or Narnia, and know it only as the birthplace of Dracula. Children may recognise it as the land where dragons live in the Harry Potter books or the

Left: *House in the Apuseni Mountains with a traditional grass roof, now a rare sight.*
Right: *Horse and cart is still a common means of transport in the country.*

country to which the Pied Piper spirited the children of Hamelin. Few of those who know that it exists could pinpoint it on a map without hesitation. Even its name has something slightly make-believe about it. Transylvania, the Latin for 'beyond the forest', is the expressive name that the Hungarians gave to a land in their domain for almost a thousand years. The Saxons who settled there in the Middle Ages called it Siebenbürgen, or Seven Citadels. None of these names would be out of place in a fairytale.

In one of their increasingly uncomfortable fireside chats, Bram Stoker's Count Dracula describes Transylvania to the narrator, Jonathan Harker, as the 'whirlpool of European races'. It is true that many peoples have occupied this land. Transylvania was fought over and longed for; it was a place where some races experienced great repression and others unimaginable freedom. Some swept over the land, usually on their way to richer pickings in the West; others settled there for centuries.

Throughout its history, Transylvania held a distinct position as a frontier zone on the border between East and West. The Carpathian Mountains form a natural boundary between the old principalities of Wallachia and Moldavia that, together with Transylvania, now make up modern-day Romania. Transylvania's archi-

Left: *View of Saxon fortified church of Aţel (Hetzeldorf), south of Mediaş (Mediasch).*
Right: *The fifteenth-century Gothic hall-church of Dârlos (Durles), with a stork's nest on the nave roof.*

tecture and its mixture of people are a product of its history as precarious border country. The Transylvanians absorbed eastern and western influences, creating something original out of them. Many people have claimed Transylvania as their own, feeling strongly that it belonged to them. The Italian academic and writer Claudio Magris describes its tangled history as 'an intricate web of disagreements, cross-purposes and clashes'. It is almost impossible to find a neutral history of Transylvania, and accounts of the origin of its inhabitants and political events vary widely, according to the author's nationality.

For most of its recorded history, Transylvania was Hungarian territory and became part of the Habsburg Empire in 1691. Its fortunes were bound up closely to those of Central Europe. Following the Austro-Hungarian Empire's collapse in 1918, it was surrendered to Romania. Romanians regard Transylvania as the 'cradle' of their culture, claiming their descent as a nation from Roman colonists and native Dacians, a branch of the Thracians, whose capital, Sarmizegetusa Regia, was in the heart of Transylvania. The Hungarians still revere Transylvania as the place where the purest forms of their culture are preserved.

Faced with such a rich array of peoples and histories, this book is selective and focuses on the Saxon towns and villages, the isolated settlements of the Apuseni and the rich traditions of Maramureş. This subjective viewpoint will no doubt be controversial – in a country that has been fought over for so long, everything is potentially contentious. The region known as Maramureş is included, which, although historically under Hungarian rule, was officially never part of Transylvania.

Transylvania is unique now in Europe, for here can be found a primal life in the forests and mountains alongside wild animals. This way of life was once common to all Europeans but is now completely lost. The region, on the very edge of Europe, seems also to be on the edge of time. It contains a link with a remote history that stretches back well into pagan times. The past hangs heavily over the land. There is something about this country that makes people yearn for it, for lost nations and empires, for a rural innocence that may never have existed.

This book portrays a way of life, miraculously preserved into the twenty-first century, that is fast disappearing. The country presented in these pages is one of rural loveliness: there are no ugly apartment blocks, polluting factories or distressing orphanages. Romania receives much negative press, and one rarely hears anything but its worst aspects.

One of the greatest surprises for the visitor to Transylvania is this sense of a place that is remarkably different, that is somehow set outside time and preserves a life and a landscape lost to the rest of Europe. This is not a recent phenomenon but one that travellers have remarked on for centuries. Even before the fictional Count Dracula had been invented in the late nineteenth century, travellers to Transylvania expressed amazement at a country that seemed not just old-fashioned but of another world. Jules Verne set his gothic novel, *A Castle in the Carpathians*, here in 1895. Emily Gerard, whose accounts of life in Transylvania in the 1880s provided inspirational background material to Bram Stoker's *Dracula*, described it as a hiding place for the super-natural, untouched by the advance of science.

Max Weber, the German sociologist, wrote about the disenchantment of the world, by which he meant that people once saw the world in which they lived as enchanted and this belief has been in decline ever since. Romania is the last place in Europe that despite, or perhaps because of, its recent past still retains some of

Left: *Lunch of fresh cheese and cream by a sheepfold.*
Following page, left: *The fourteenth-century Saxon church of Hălmeag (Halmagen).*
Following page, right: *Part of the 12m high defensive wall at the Saxon church of Prejmer (Tartlau), begun before the Mongol invasion of 1241.*

Right: *Romanian Orthodox church at Troaş. The Romanians in Transylvania, lacking the wealth and power to build in stone, constructed their churches out of wood.*
Far right: *Buffalo are used for transport and milk in Romania. In recent years, some British farmers have bought Romanian buffalo because their milk, used to make mozzarella cheese, commands a good price.*

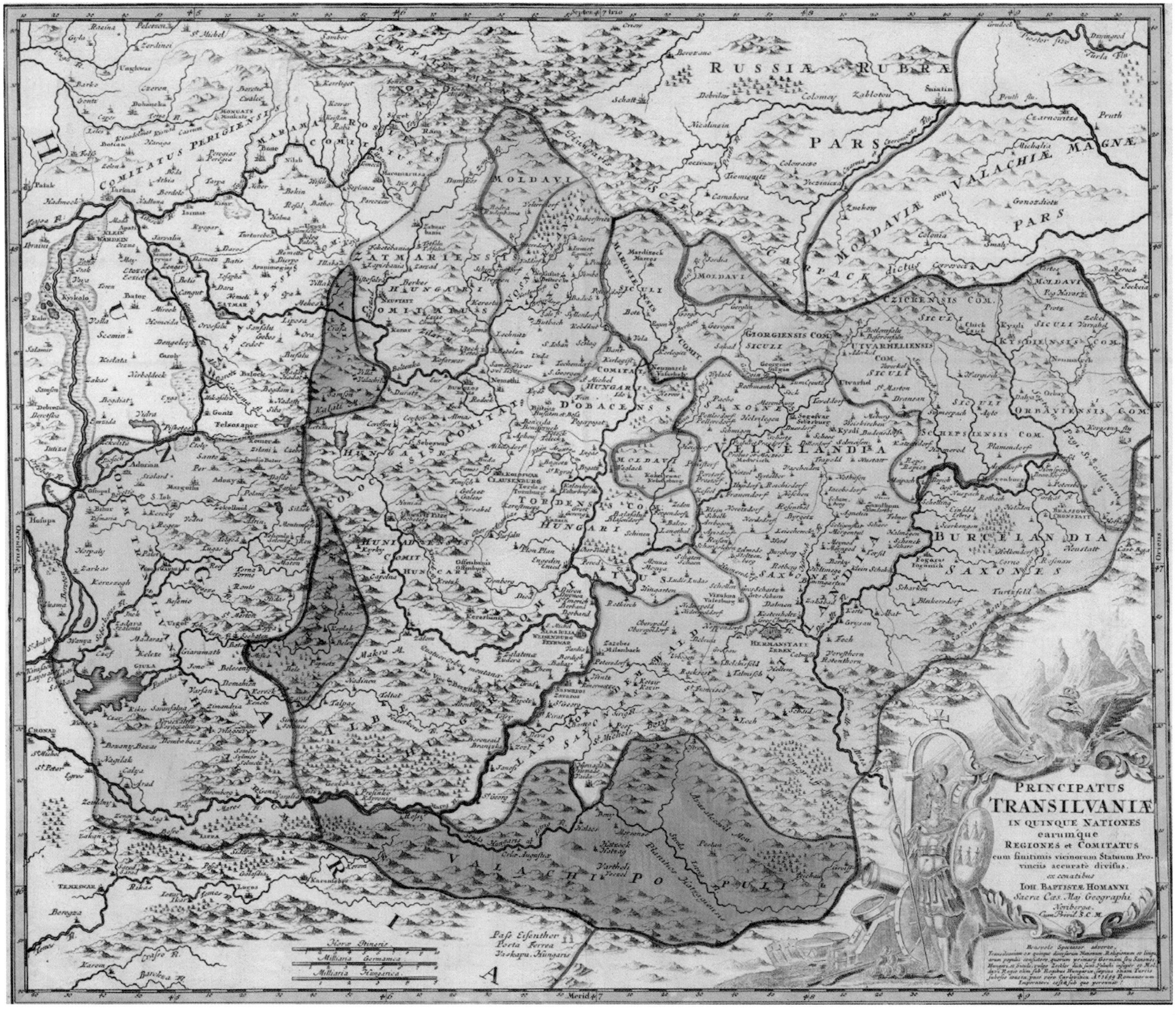
PRINCIPATUS
TRANSILVANIÆ
IN QUINQUE NATIONES
earumque
REGIONES et COMITATUS
cum finitimis vicinorum Statuum Provinciis accurate divisus.
ex conatibus
IOH. BAPTISTÆ HOMANNI
Sacræ Cæs. Maj. Geographi
Norimbergæ.
Cum Privil. S.C.M.
RUSSIÆ RUBRÆ
PARS
MOLDAVIÆ seu VALACHIÆ MAGNÆ
PARS
CARPACK dictus
COMITATUS PERIGIENSIS
MARAMAROS COMITATUS
ZATMARIENSIS
HUNGARI
VINELANDIA
BURCELANDIA
SAXONES
DOBACENSIS
TORDENSIS COMIT.
HUNGARI
HUNIADENSIS COMIT.
HUNGARI
ALBENSIS
VALACHI POPULI
Horæ Itineris
Milliaria Germanica
Milliaria Hungarica

that magic. There is only a hint of it now, in remote villages and in the mountains and forests. Visitors saw this magical, fragile world already under threat a century ago, warning that the traditions, superstitions and even parts of the population itself were in danger of extinction. Somehow that world struggled on through two World Wars. It was kept artificially alive by the great economic failure of Communism. Now capitalism and membership of the European Union will wipe out in a handful of years what Communism failed to do in nearly 50.

The disappearance of the Saxon population has been one of Transylvania's great losses. Less than a year after the Romanian revolution of December 1989, three-quarters of the Transylvanian Saxons returned to Germany, almost 900 years after their arrival. Right up to that time, they had preserved dress, customs and a dialect that would have been more familiar to Hans Holbein in the sixteenth century than to a modern-day German. It was no wonder that some people thought the Pied Piper had spirited away the children of Hamelin to Transylvania.

Left: *Map of Transylvania by John Baptist Homann, about 1720, showing the division of territory between Hungarians, Szeklers and Saxons, with small pockets under Moldavian and Wallachian rule.*

Now mainly the old are left and the sight of anyone in traditional dress is rare, although a visitor to a Saxon church may still hear the occasional greeting of Grüss Gott from a Saxon who chose to stay behind. Although so many have gone, their extraordinary fortified churches and villages remain, as does the surrounding countryside with a rich diversity of wildflowers, birds, insects and animals that was lost in Western Europe years ago. The dilemma now is what to do with a precious European landscape largely untouched by the modern age.

The photographs by Dan Dinescu in this book capture lives of great simplicity in a setting of unimaginable beauty. Transylvania has an unmistakable allure as a mysterious place where uncommon things happen. Here one can still find characters from a pre-industrial landscape, familiar now only from history books and childhood tales. It is a world of all our pasts, reassuringly familiar yet thrillingly different.

***Left:** The Carpathian Mountains offered Transylvania some protection against invasion from the east.*

Chapter 1

The Pied Piper's Children

Among the great curiosities of Transylvania are the Saxon towns, villages and fortified churches. The Germans who settled here from the twelfth century gave much of this area its distinctive flavour. So strange a phenomenon it seemed, these stolid Germans with their orderly houses and neat customs transplanted into an exotic land – this 'imaginative whirlpool', as Jonathan Harker writes in *Dracula* – that as early as the sixteenth century a link was made with the lost children of Hamelin who disappeared from the German town in the thirteenth century. The story reached a popular audience through the Grimm brothers in their *Deutsche Sagen* (German Legends, 1816–18), and was made famous throughout the English-speaking world by Robert Browning's poem, *The Pied Piper of Hamelin* (1842).

According to the legend recorded by Grimm, in 1284 a mysterious man dressed in many colours appeared in the town of Hamelin. He claimed that he could rid the town of a plague of rats in return for an agreed sum of money. As soon as the man started to blow on a small pipe, rats came pouring out of every nook and cranny, scurrying towards him. He led them to the river where they all drowned. But when the piper asked the citizens for the money they had promised him, they failed to keep their part of the bargain and refused to pay. The piper went away quietly but returned to Hamelin on the Feast of St Peter and St Paul,

wearing the dress of a huntsman and a peculiar red hat. He did not look in the least bit friendly this time.

Again, he took the pipe out of his pocket, but now when he played it, the town's children appeared and crowded round him. He led them outside the town and into a mountain, where they disappeared. Only three children were saved – a blind one, a mute, and a little boy who had run back to fetch his jacket. The parents searched high and low for their children, sending messages out to all corners of the land, but no one saw or heard of the children again. Robert Browning takes up the story:

... in Transylvania there's a tribe
Of alien people that ascribe
The outlandish ways and dress
On which their neighbours lay such stress,
To their fathers and mother having risen
Out of some subterraneous prison
Into which they were trepanned
Long time ago in a mighty band
Out of Hamelin town in Brunswick land ...

Many theories have been advanced to explain the legend and the fate of the missing children, including suggestions that the piper was recruiting for the Children's Crusade, that tragic expedition to the Holy Land on which thousands of children embarked from France and the Rhineland in 1212, never to return. Others suggest that he was a metaphor for a plague that carried the children away. Certainly, the image of a sinister figure luring people to their deaths would have been a familiar one, for the *Dance of Death*, or *Danse macabre*, was a common theme in church wall paintings. In France and England, Death is usually depicted as a skeleton armed with a scythe, spade or a spear; however, in Germany, the musical aspect of the dance is emphasised, and the Devil is often shown playing the pipes. The rats seem to be a later addition, and the earliest accounts do not mention them.

By the sixteenth century, rats had made their appearance in the story, together with the proposal that the children were taken to Transylvania. Richard Verstegan, whose *Restitution of Decayed Intelligence in Antiquities* (1605) was the earliest known account in English of the children's disappearance, adds that among the Saxons of Transylvania there are people with the same surnames as those in Hamelin, which would suggest that the 'Jugler or Pi'd Piper might have transported them there by Necromancy'. He gives no examples and concludes that this theory has no credibility, for 'it would have been almost as great a wonder to the Saxons of Transylvania to have had so many strange children brought amongst them, as it were to those of Hamelin to lose them, and they could not but have kept memory of such a strange thing, if indeed any such thing had happened'.

As the Saxons were quite exceptionally careful with all their possessions and kept meticulous archives, it would indeed have been surprising if they had failed to record the sudden appearance of 130 children accompanied by a mysterious piper in a fantastical coat. But the earliest history of their settlement in Transylvania is in fact disappointingly meagre, and there is no evidence of any specific group of settlers arriving from one particular town in any of their histories.

Other accounts of the origins of the Transylvanian Saxons were being discussed in the seventeenth century. Like the Romanians in later centuries, the Saxons were able to see the advantages of tracing an unbroken lineage from the Dacians, the first recorded settlers in the region, which would establish a presence in Transylvania that predated the Hungarians. Johannes Tröster's *Das alt- und neu-teutsche Dacia* (The Old and New German Dacia), published in 1666 and one of the first comprehensive histories of the Transylvanian

Left: *Girl running across the street in the Saxon fortified town of Sighişoara.*

306

Saxons, repeats an idea first proposed by Renaissance writers that they were descended from the Dacians, who were direct descendants of the German Goths and Thracian Getae. According to this, the term 'Saxon' came from Daken – Saken – Sachsen. Several prominent Saxons took up this theory with enthusiasm, and it gained wide acceptance until being quietly dropped at some point in the eighteenth century.

In earlier centuries, only Transylvania was mentioned as a possible destination for the lost children of Hamelin, but more recent theories have traced the children to other areas of Central and Eastern Europe, such as Moravia (now part of the Czech Republic). The Pied Piper, it is claimed, was recruiting young men and women – rather than very young children – to settle underpopulated lands to the east. Like Verstegan, several modern researchers have sought to trace the children by comparing family and place names, and Jürgen Udolph, a linguist at Leipzig University, recently concluded from such a study that they had settled in the state of Brandenburg, north and north-east of Berlin. Radu Florescu suggested in his book, *In Search of the Pied Piper*, that the children were taken away to be settlers in the newly formed Baltic states but lost at sea.

Looking today at these German towns and villages transplanted so far from their homeland, the theory that a plausible stranger recruited young people to emigrate there from Hamelin at the end of the thirteenth century does not seem entirely ludicrous. The Saxon villages and towns could certainly illustrate Browning's poem perfectly. Resolutely German yet strangely unreal and remote, they are a nineteenth-century romantic's idea of the Middle Ages. Soaring over each settlement is the fortified church. The medieval Saxons were free men, so they defended their own church, not a nobleman's castle. In a typical Saxon village, the houses – built in the same style for centuries – line each side of a mud-baked street. A stream, shaded by apple and chestnut trees, cuts through the centre of the village while ducks, geese and the odd turkey waddle along its banks. Brightly dressed gypsies inhabit the margins of the village, while in the surrounding fields men work their strips of land with ploughs and scythes and boys herd goats in the hills. In

Left: *Many of the medieval fortifications survive in the former Saxon capital of Sibiu (Hermannstadt).*
Right: *Street scene in Sibiu. Note the windows in the roof – the 'eyes' of the city.*
Previous page, left: *Horse and cart outside a crumbling Saxon house in Saschiz (Keisd).*
Previous page, right: *Tending a model vegetable garden. The Saxons' sense of orderliness is much missed.*

the distance are the snow-peaked Carpathians, home to bears and wolves. But, as with all fairytales, beyond the first magical view, sometimes less pleasant things lurk.

On closer inspection, the green paint on some of the village houses is peeling. Flies gorge on the plums in the church orchard because there are so few left to pick the fruit. The culture that sustained this life for a thousand years – the traditions and superstitions, the food, dress and language that survived the invaders, two World Wars and years of Communism – has almost vanished in one generation.

More than 800 years ago, from about 1143, the Hungarian King Géza II invited groups referred to as *hospites Teutonici et Flandrenses* – German and Flemish guests – to settle within the arc of the Carpathians. In return, they were expected to cultivate and defend the land against the semi-nomadic tribes of Tatars and Cumans that regularly devastated the area. The Saxons called their land Siebenbürgen, possibly after the seven great castles that they built, and their most important town was Hermannstadt, now called Sibiu.

In 1211, when Transylvania was again under threat from Cumans and Tatars who had settled as far west as northern Moldavia, King Andrew II granted a charter to the Teutonic Knights, an order which had been founded in 1189 during the Third Crusade, to defend the land and convert the

pagan enemy to Catholicism. He gave them the south-eastern region of Transylvania, around Braşov, known as the Burzenland. But their Grand Master angered the king by encouraging Pope Honorius III to take the Burzenland under his direct control, and so Andrew expelled them from the Kingdom of Hungary. They then removed to the Baltic state that became Prussia.

The German and Flemish settlers proved to be more grateful and trustworthy guests, and in 1224 Andrew granted them complete self-government under an elected leader, known as the *Sachsengraf*, or Saxon Count, who was answerable only to the Hungarian king. In return, the Saxons, as they were called, agreed to fulfil certain military obligations. They were given the right to elect their own judges and clergy; they had exclusive property rights and their merchants were exempt from tolls and dues throughout the kingdom. These were extraordinarily beguiling terms in a feudal age and great incentives to stay in the face of the threat from the east.

Most of the original settlers appear to have come from the area of the Moselle in Frankenland, and it is not clear how they came to be known as Saxons, although they had received this name by 1204. Their dialect, which those who remain in Transylvania still speak, is said to be more intelligible to the inhabitants of rural Luxembourg than to modern Germans. The privileges granted to them made them the political equals of the Hungarian nobility and the Szeklers, who settled mainly on the eastern frontier; together they were recognised as the three privileged nations. The Hungarian-speaking Szeklers consider themselves an ancient branch of the Huns who settled in Transylvania in the fifth century and did not withdraw to the east after the death of Attila in 453, as did their fellow Hungarians.

By the fifteenth century, the Saxons had organised the four regions in which they had settled – centring on Braşov (Kronstadt), Sibiu (Hermannstadt), Mediaş (Mediasch) and Bistriţa (Bistritz) – into one representative body called the *Nationuniversität*, with their elected leader. He was the guarantor of their independence, and the Saxons managed to cling onto this privilege until 1876, when the role was abolished by the Hungarian government.

The area in which the Saxons settled is a land of low-lying hills and pasture. Writers like to compare this countryside of gentle hills and villages nestled around a church with England as it was 100 or 200 years ago. But the Saxon villages are not English. They are more like Hamelin or Nuremberg, belonging not to the landscape of Constable or Cotman but to that of Dürer or Altdorfer. English villages do not proclaim themselves; their gentle modesty is an expression of their security. The Saxon villages, their houses painted green, ochre or pale blue, are charming, but the peppery redness of their undulating rooftops and the massive towers and walls of their churches look prickly.

The Saxons brought their industry, economy and religion to the easternmost edges of Europe. They were granted great freedom and they had no truck with the aristocracy. The most important structure in each of their towns and villages was the church, and it was the church that replaced the nobleman's castle as a focus of defence in times of war. The architecture of their houses, while attractive in its simplicity, is also rather forbidding. To the casual observer, the houses seem to run in a continuous united row along either side of the road. But they do not have front doors opening onto the street. A massive gate, as high as the wall of the house, entirely blocks off any view of the house and the inner courtyard. All the houses, even those dating from the 1960s, are in the same style, built straight onto the road with red-tiled Dutch gables. To gain admittance, the visitor must pass through a small door cut into the entrance gate. As with the churches, the Saxons designed their houses to keep themselves and their privileges secure, and to keep foreigners out. Behind the tall gates is everything a

Left: The 16th-17th century defensive walls of the aptly named 'white church' at Viscri (Deutschweißkirch).

family needs to survive day-to-day life. The houses have large cellars for storing food and drink during the winter. Vines grow around the door; beyond the house, still contained within the walls and fences, are a summer kitchen, a vegetable and flower garden, pens for chickens and housing for a pig, a cow and sheep. A barn and an orchard beyond complete the household.

The size and architectural ambition of the Saxon houses and churches reveal a wealth and confidence that the native Romanian villages lacked. The Romanians built mostly in wood because they were too poor to build in stone, and lacked the resources to defend themselves effectively. They were so permanently afraid their villages would be attacked that they even at times in some parts of the country constructed their churches on wheels so they could be moved to safer ground when the enemy came. This is an exercise they were forced to repeat in the 1980s, when the Communist President Ceauşescu's brutal plans to demolish a large portion of historic Bucharest threatened some of the city's oldest churches. The sixteenth-century Mihai Voda church was lifted onto wheels and trundled a few metres down the road where it was obscured by apartment blocks.

Traditional Romanian houses do not reveal the same obsession with locking people out. They have entrance gates – in some areas, such as Maramureş, often very elaborate – but the house and courtyard are always visible, so there is always a link with the outside world. Hungarian rural settlements are again quite different, displaying what one writer called a 'formal simplicity'. Even the large elaborate gates found among the Szeklers usually have one low adjoining wall which looks into the courtyard. Although some of the Szekler churches have defensive walls around them, they do not approach the scale or sophistication of the Saxon fortifications.

The Saxons built their churches on high ground where possible and surrounded them with walls and towers. In some of the churches they planted fruit trees within the grounds; others had larders for each family in the village to lay by provisions for difficult times. These rooms have been preserved impressively at Prejmer (Tartlau) and Hărman (Honigberg). Many kept stores of grain in large wooden boxes placed in orderly rows around inner walls that were protected from rain and missiles by projecting wooden roofs. Often, there was a well either within the fortifications or even in the church itself, as at Bod (Brenndorf) and Merghindeal (Mergeln); also included were millstones and bread ovens. Every church had a *Speckturm*, a tower in which the villagers hung sides of ham. It was safer to keep it there in case the Cumans, the Tatars or the Turks came.

Elizabeth Kyle, a Scottish writer who visited Transylvania before the Second World War, recounted how, while looking round the Saxon fortified church at Hărman, she had seen hams that were green with age. 'Why are such old hams hanging there?' she asked a young Saxon woman, who told her that the ancient hams were about 200 years old.

'Because, *Dank sei Gott*,' came the reply, 'there has been no siege. They were not needed.'

This story captured my imagination, and it became my ambition to find a ham hanging in such a bacon tower – and preferably a Saxon woman wearing traditional dress still heedful of the possibility of siege. Someone who was proudly aware that her culture originated 2,000 kilometres west and who, among a people profoundly different from her, steadfastly maintained her customs and language and mouldy old hams after 800 years.

The superb fortifications of the thirteenth-century church at Hărman – two ring walls, seven towers and a moat – were an essential precaution for an area under constant threat. Although the village was burned several times during its history, the church held fast, even against such terrifying onslaughts as the occasion when, in 1658, a group of Turks, Tatars, Wallachians, Moldavians and Cossacks plundered the region. Living and store rooms for each family in the village to use in times of siege were built into the inner defensive wall. Although these store rooms still exist on the south side and have recently been restored, they no longer contain any trace of food, neither bread nor ham. When I asked the church custodian, a Saxon and a keen local historian, whether he thought it possible that the people would have stored their hams for centuries without ever eating them, he was perplexed by the suggestion. He said that until the majority of Saxons left in 1990, they had continued to store hams within the church walls but they had cut slices off the meat every Sunday for their weekly use. They would not have let good meat go to waste.

A custodian at neighbouring Prejmer was similarly puzzled. After some careful consideration, she recalled that after cutting a loaf of bread, her grandmother would sweep all the crumbs into a drawer under the kitchen table; at the end of each week she would collect them up and use them to make schnitzel. This was the only instance where she could think of anyone saving old food. But her grandmother never wasted a crumb and certainly would not have allowed anything she produced to go mouldy.

Right: *The 1814 arcaded walkway over the former drawbridge at Hărman (Honigberg). Its defences withstood numerous attacks, including an invasion of Turks, Tatars, Moldavians and Cossacks in 1658.*

After the disappointment of finding so many empty store cupboards, I headed for Biertan (Birthälm). In its heyday, Biertan was an important place, a seat of Protestant bishops for 300 years, and I was hopeful that it would have ample bacon towers to reflect its position. The road to Biertan felt foreign because it is straight and flimsy wooden fences divide the fields. The village is eight kilometres away from the nearest railway station, and the first time I visited on foot. The road passed first through an old Saxon settlement called Şaroş pe Târnave (Scharosch), which contained a fortified church. There was an enticing covered walkway leading up to it, but the entrance was locked. Never able to pass by a fortified church, I left the path to explore the walls and at once a little group of laughing, begging gypsy children surrounded me. '*Străina, străina*,' they hissed to themselves: 'foreigner, foreigner.' I had been so busy

Left: *The late Gothic church at Biertan (Birthälm) dominates the surrounding countryside. From 1572 to 1867 it was the seat of the Transylvanian Saxon bishops and several of their elaborate gravestones are preserved.*
Previous page, left: *Saxon village of Biertan. Plots of land rise up the hillside behind the houses.*
Previous page, right: *Saxon street at Meşendorf (Meschendorf). Only five old Saxons remain in the village.*

looking at the church exterior that I had not noticed the path led to a small gypsy settlement, little more than a group of tiny broken-down huts. I had no business there. Foolish stranger to leave the straight road.

Apple trees lined the road through a valley of small maize fields, divided by ditches and wooden fences that stretched up on either side to a low ridge of hills, partly forested. Except for a couple of crows circling above the woods, there was no sign of life until I met an old gypsy woman on the outskirts of Biertan. She was wearing the most popular skirt for gypsies in Transylvania that year: a bright red tartan with stiff pleats. In one hand, although it was a cold day, she held her pinched black shoes. Her feet were hurting, she said, and although she carried a large bag on her other arm, this hand remained cupped, as if it were made that way, created to beg.

From a distance, the church looked like an enormous rocky outcrop on the side of a hill. Slowly it began to take shape, until the soaring towers and walls of the late Gothic church were visible. Seeing it come into view for the first time along that long straight road, it had the same impact as Chartres Cathedral in the way in which it dominated the surrounding landscape.

It was early afternoon in Biertan. A couple of dusty children, with clothes as shabby as the houses in which they lived, were playing outside in the cold winter sun. They were absorbed in their game and ignored me. The approach to the church was by the west side of the main square. Although the gatekeeper and his family, who lived in a room off the covered entrance passage, spoke German, they were not Saxons. The custodian, a Romanian, had learned the language at the local school, and now that almost all the Saxons in Biertan had left for Germany, he looked after the church and acted as a guide.

Here, as all over Siebenbürgen, the Saxons had gone following the overthrow of the Ceauşescu regime in December 1989; half of those who left did so in the first six months. When I asked Friedrich Gunesch, the bishop's secretary in Sibiu, how it could have happened so quickly, he replied: 'Their suitcases were already packed, and in many families they had been packed for years.'

The revolution precipitated an exodus that had been taking place for almost a century. The first Saxons to return to Germany in any number were the inhabitants of a group of wine-making villages, whose vines were killed by weevils at the beginning of the twentieth century. The Saxons' privileges and status had eroded gradually under Austro-Hungarian rule. Following the creation in 1867 of the Dual Monarchy between Austria and Hungary, the Transylvanian Diet, or assembly, was abolished, ending the centuries-old rule of the privileged nations. It was a bitter blow as thereafter Transylvania was ruled from Budapest and Hungarian became the official language. The abolition of the ancient office of Saxon Count was the final humiliation. By this time, however, the Saxons were already a spent force as a nation, with a dwindling population vastly outnumbered by the Hungarians and Romanians.

After the defeat of Germany in the First World War and the break-up of the Austro-Hungarian Empire, the Treaty of Trianon in 1920 rewarded Romania, which had finally joined the winning side in 1916, with the longed-for prize of Transylvania. While this further eroded Saxon confidence, the terms of the treaty had a far more profound effect on Hungary, which lost half its population and two-thirds of its territory, one-third of which was in Transylvania. The Hungarian nobility were forced to surrender large portions of their estates, and minor officials of the old regime lost their jobs to Romanians.

In 1920, there were approximately 400,000 Lutherans in Transylvania; by 1949, that number had halved. The Saxons suffered great losses during the two World Wars. An estimated 175,000 ethnic Germans were killed or left the country during the Second World War, and many died in the deportations to Russia in 1947. Within 15 years of the 1989 revolution, there were only about 14,000 Saxons left, most of whom were elderly.

After the Second World War, some Saxons who had

fought for the Germans remained in Germany or Austria, and at the start of the 1950s, a few wives and children were able to join them through the *Familienzusammenführung*, an organisation set up to reunite families split up during the war. As the Communist regime in Romania became more repressive, however, such opportunities became increasingly difficult.

In the same way that Ceaușescu granted exit visas to members of Romania's Jewish community in exchange for dollars, so he came to an agreement with Chancellor Schmidt in 1978 to sell his ethnic Germans for Deutschmarks. The West German government paid several thousand Deutschmarks per person for some 12,000–16,000 exit permits each year. The Saxons who left during this time could only take with them what they could carry, and the state expropriated their houses, allowing the gypsies to settle in them, an act which incensed Saxon and Romanian alike. The gypsies suffer from high rates of unemployment, illiteracy and crime, and with their population now thought to be greater than that of the ethnic Hungarians, they represent one of Romania's most serious social problems.

Prejudice against gypsies manifests itself in different ways at every level of society. 'Gypsy' is a term of abuse and synonymous with the word thief. Everyone seems to know at least one 'decent' gypsy, yet as a group they are widely condemned. Many people admire their music. Others favour them for their fortune-telling or skill at metal work. Since the revolution, the standard of living of most gypsies has decreased, and many are now dependent once more on making a living from traditional crafts and skills, and from begging.

Gypsies have led a precarious life on the margins of society – as they have done throughout Europe – since their first recorded appearance in Romania in 1385, when several families are listed among the property of a monastery. Gypsies were enslaved in Wallachia and Moldavia right up to the 1850s, but their status in Transylvania differed considerably. Although gypsies who lived on lands owned by Wallachian princes within Transylvania were slaves, in Hungarian territory they had the status of serfs, while those in the area under Saxon control lived as free men on the outskirts of villages and towns. Gypsies performed certain 'unclean' jobs in the Transylvanian towns, acting as executioners, latrine cleaners and road sweepers, and are still commonly employed in these last two jobs. Others traditionally worked sifting gold, making or laying bricks, and as copperworkers. Nomadic gypsies would winter on a nobleman's estate but travel round the country in the summer, in the way that contemporary travelling circuses continue to do.

The gypsies had their own hierarchy. In the sixteenth century a gypsy voivode, or prince, was rewarded for services to Sibiu with gifts of Turkish rugs and silver. In later centuries, records of local gypsy princes emerge. The Emperor of Rom from Everywhere still lives on the outskirts of Sibiu in a gigantic oriental-looking palace with silver turrets and several hundred rooms. His rival, the King of the Rom, lives in a similarly extravagant palace near Alba Iulia. Although most gypsies live below the poverty line, a few families have flourished in the entrepreneurial free-for-all since the revolution. When the gypsies make money, they tend to build large flamboyant houses and literally flash their money around. Many Romanians resent such displays of wealth, which they suspect is due to dishonest activity.

Although it is now generally accepted that the gypsies came to Europe from India, no one knows exactly how or when they did so. They are thought to have left the subcontinent in successive waves and to have first entered Persia in the tenth century, possibly as a caste of travelling musicians. The circumstances of their enslavement in Romania are also mysterious. One theory is that the gypsies were prisoners of war of the Tatars during the Mongol invasions in the thirteenth century and were taken as spoils of war after the Tatars were defeated. Another suggestion is that they were enslaved at a time of economic crisis when the land was depopulated by war and there was a need for cheap labour.

During the 1770s and 1780s under the Habsburg Empress Maria Theresa and Emperor Joseph II, attempts to settle the gypsy population and turn them into 'New Hungarians' met with limited success, although by the nineteenth century most Transylvanian gypsies were sedentary. During the Communist era the 'gypsy question' was ignored, and they were not recognised as a separate ethnic group.

It would be hard to think of a people more unlike the ponderous, fair-skinned Saxons with their Protestant northern values than the gypsies. 'We have one or two children and work,' one Saxon said bitterly. 'Gypsies

Right: *Gypsy family selling a copper still for making plum brandy by the side of the road near Mediaş (Mediasch). They belong to a traditional caste of gypsies called Kalderash, or cauldron makers.*
Following page, left: *Garden belonging to a gypsy family in a small settlement outside Viscri. The colourful, carefully tended garden stood out in a place where many people lived in the squalid conditions of deep poverty.*
Following page, right: *Gypsies charcoal-burning. They will use the fuel to smelt iron. Many gypsies scratch a living by such traditional and time-consuming activities.*

have 15 children and don't work and the state subsidises them, gives them our money for not working, and when we leave, gives them our houses.'

Transylvania lives by its own particular rhythm where time does not seem to move at the same rate as elsewhere, so it is no surprise to learn that writers were already foretelling the imminent demise of the Saxon people 150 years ago on account of their low birth rate. 'How is it that these German colonists, all thinking men, should thus dwindle away, instead of peopling the land with their race?' asked Charles Boner in the mid-nineteenth century. He described villages that were once purely Saxon 'with but a few Wallack huts outside the boundary', now being almost entirely populated by 'Wallacks', or ethnic Romanians. In another village he found a German Protestant church where the congregation consisted of just one family. Boner ascribed this to the 'merited retribution for a heavy offence against nature and morality', by which he meant that the Saxons practised birth control so they could keep their house and land intact and avoid their estate being divided up among too many children. It took 150 years for Boner's fears to be realised, although not in quite the same way as he imagined. The Saxons abandoned their land to seek a life of greater material comfort in Germany, where they thought that their children would have a better future.

Left: *Herr Dootz, still chopping wood and drawing his own water at the age of 101. He stayed in Transylvania in 1989, although most of his family left for Germany.*

Now the remaining Saxons and also the Romanians who live in the former Saxon villages are afraid that they will be soon be outnumbered by gypsies. Just as the Romanians had once lived in huts on the outside of Saxon villages, so the gypsies now occupy a similar position, although many also now live in the Saxons' old houses. Birth control is still an issue as it was in the nineteenth century, but this time it is the fact that the gypsies do not tend to practise it that causes moral outrage.

A young man who showed us around another church and who was hoping to go to Germany as soon as he left school said that the gypsies had vandalised the church. He called them 'Tatars', an insult that was doubly interesting because it was the name of his people's ancient enemy and also because of the theory that the gypsies had first come into Romania as slaves of the Tatars. The boy knew nothing about the etymology of the insult, simply that everyone in the village had always called the gypsies Tatars.

On the way down from the church, we met a good-looking gypsy boy, aged 16, the eldest of 11 children. He was proud of the fact that he had a job working in the forest for £60 a month. I asked him how old his mother was.

'She's an old woman,' he replied.

'How old?'

'38 years.'

'And how old is your father?'

'60,' but he did not call him an old man.

Gypsies tend to have much larger families than average. Women often marry very young, even below the age of 16, and couples do not always use any contraception. Large families are expensive, of course, and a very high proportion of children in orphanages come from a gypsy background – sometimes as high as 90 per cent – sent there because their parents can no longer afford to keep them. The majority of gypsies are desperately poor, with up to 80 per cent living below the poverty line, and some 60 per cent under the minimum subsistence level.

'It's hard for the Saxons in Germany,' said Laura, a Romanian student from Sighişoara (Schässburg) who had a Saxon boyfriend. 'There are about 300,000 of them there now, but they are not always accepted. They might speak German, but because they are Romanian, people think they are gypsies. But they don't feel Romanian, either.'

'Why should they be treated like gypsies?' I asked.

'Oh, come on, everyone in Europe thinks the Romanians are gypsies, don't they? You know the story about the swans in Vienna?'

'No.'

'Oh, don't say they don't know about it in Britain. A few years ago, some Romanian gypsies caught a couple of swans on the Danube in Vienna and ate them, and that is the impression people have of us. Of all of us.'

One of the early editions of a guidebook to Romania published in the 1990s had a band of gypsy musicians on its front cover, with Romania written in large letters underneath it. To the western publishers and to the book's readers, the photograph was an understandable choice – gypsy musicians were a picturesque aspect of Romania's heritage. It was only when the picture was met with disapproving looks in Romania that I realised how much offence it caused. For the average Romanian, it was the equivalent of choosing a photograph of social delinquents to illustrate a guidebook to a Western European country.

Many foreigners, quite understandably, imagine that the words 'Romania' and 'Romany' must be linked in some way, an observation to make most Romanians spit hot words of indignation. The Romanians proudly called themselves so, because they believed themselves to be a Latin race and to emphasise their connections with the Romans. The gypsies called themselves Rom – the name by which they preferred to be known because of the negative connotations of the word gypsy, from the word meaning a 'man', as opposed to a 'gadjo' or foreigner: that is, anyone who is not a Rom.

At the church in Biertan I met a Saxon woman in her early 60s who had gone to live with her family near Munich, and I asked her how she found life there.

'Mm,' she replied in an unenthusiastic voice, 'I like it.'

'Is it better than here?'

She gave an indeterminate little nod and pouted her lips, as if to say, not really.

The German government, which happily issued all ethnic Germans from the former Soviet bloc with entry visas, was taken by surprise at the huge number that came so quickly. In an effort to curb emigration, the Germans gave aid to the Saxon community, sending donations of farm machinery and assistance for cultural projects. The German government supports the Saxon political party, the German Democratic Forum, which is represented in the Romanian Parliament. Until very recently, there have been only a few cases of young people making money in Germany and returning to invest in Romania, and an entire generation of children with Saxon parents has now grown up in Germany. There have been some success stories. One of the sons of 100-year-old Johann Dootz, who still lived alone in the house he had built himself, chopping wood for his fire and drawing his water from a spring in the garden, had returned to Transylvania. Like Johann, his son was a builder by trade, and there was now such increased demand for construction that he could make a decent living in Romania, with more work than he could manage. Herr Dootz put this down to the fact that it was because he was an honest Saxon who knew how to work hard and work well.

Some Saxons have managed to reclaim their property – confiscated during Communist times – and now use their former houses as holiday homes or have converted them into hotels and guesthouses that set a standard for others to follow. The remote village of Viscri (Weißkirchdorf) has become a model for successful eco-tourism in the area, one of the real hopes for the rural economy, largely thanks to the efforts of Caroline Fernolend, a young Saxon woman who decided to stay in her ancestral village with her husband and daughter. She and her neighbours have opened their homes as

Right: *Herr Verner striding through Meşendorf. He still cares for the church at the age of 96. He survived the war and deportations and ran the local collective farm.*

Gott ist die Liebe
Der treuste Führer in der Not.
Das ist und bleibt der liebe Gott.
Zwei Lebenstützen brechen nie
Gebet und Arbeit heissen sie.
Gehst du im Leben einst hinaus
Lobe den Herren meine Seele
und vergiss nicht,
was er dir Gutes getan hat
Wie die Tage
so die Kraft

guesthouses and have plans to produce organic food to sell. She has made efforts to integrate the gypsies in her plans for the regeneration of the village, and, as mayor, employed them to make wicker baskets for use as litter bins on the street and to knit socks and hats to sell to visitors.

In the old Saxon capital of Sibiu, where the Saxons make up only 1.6 per cent of the city's population, a Saxon mayor and member of the German Democratic Forum, Klaus Johannis, was re-elected as mayor for a second four-year term in 2004. 'Everyone respects him,' a Romanian said. 'It takes a Saxon to sort out this mess.' The Romanians who lived in the former Saxon towns evidently missed the Saxons once they had gone. 'You should have seen this place when the Saxons lived here,' a Romanian woman reminisced in one town. 'It was so clean and tidy with so many flowers. Every house had window boxes and flowers in the courtyard. But now. Pah!' she snorted. *'Mizerie!'* (This is a brilliantly expressive – and frequently used –word for a mess and wretchedness in general.) Romanians had no sense of housekeeping, she went on, and gypsies even less. In the beautiful but decaying village of Roadeş (Radeln), gypsy faces peered out from the dirty windows of the former Saxon houses on the main street. All the once handsome buildings that had been the centre of the community – the priest's house, school and kindergarten – were vandalised and falling into ruin. A Saxon woman who showed us round the church told us sadly: 'Between what it once was and what it is now, there is no comparison.'

Left: ***Frau Krӓch, one of a handful of Saxons left in her village – all her children have gone to Germany – she is the only one still to wear traditional Saxon dress and to preserve a traditional Saxon interior in her house.***

Their distinctive culture is commemorated now only in museums and exhibitions, and at the annual reunions, when Saxons return from Germany to their native villages to meet up with friends, family and former neighbours and to celebrate their old way of life. The answer to questions about Saxon dress, art or furniture was always the same: they can only be seen in museums. The best place to go to learn about Saxon culture now, I was told, was the Saxon library and archive at Schloss Hornech in Gundelsheim, near Heilbronn in Germany.

In Transylvania, the churches and houses are still standing, but there are only vague hints of the life that once was lived within them, caught in chance meetings and conversations with some of those who are left. By good fortune, in a remote village outside Sibiu, I found a woman in her early seventies who maintained at least the outward appearance of her traditional life. She was wearing a shirt with fine smocking, which still gleamed white and clean even though it was the middle of a weekday and she had been feeding her chickens in the yard. When I complimented her on the shirt and asked if she still wore Saxon dress on a Sunday, to my delight she said that she would show me her traditional clothes. She asked me into her house and the best room, the one traditionally reserved for visitors where she kept her prize possessions.

I had only ever seen such a room in a museum. It made me realise how artificial such recreations often are, with artefacts artfully arranged in a moment of time that never existed, any contemporary article of mass production carefully discarded and only 'tasteful' exhibits on display. Here in Frau Krӓch's best room were treasures amassed and carefully preserved until the present day. Together with the traditional embroidery patterns of fruit and flowers in sober black stitches was a cushion embroidered with a jolly red robin which could have come from anywhere in the West. Hanging alongside the religious and improving texts on the wall was a plastic clock in the shape of a giant gold Rolex watch. This clock is ubiquitous throughout the country. It first came to Romania just after the revolution, and swiftly became one of the most widely available and desirable items in the countryside, a gigantic symbol of glitzy western consumerism after years of rationing, when even basic items such as soap, flour and toothpaste had been in short supply. Inside a glass case, of the sort in one which usually finds Victorian stuffed birds, were two dolls in Saxon costume that looked as though they had been captured under their glass capsule at some time during the 1970s. It was hard to tell in which decades the black and white framed photographs had been taken, for the people in the 1930s were wearing identical dress to those in the 1960s and 70s; only an examination of hairstyles told them apart.

Yet the room preserved all its traditional aspects. It would have been recognisable to a Saxon in the nineteenth or even eighteenth century, with handmade furniture, painted jugs in a neat row above the window ledge, white linen painstakingly embroidered, decorative pillows piled above tall 'cupboard' beds, the base of which was a drawer for storage or for a child to sleep in. Embroidered texts on the walls cautioned and comforted the inhabitants of the house:

Sorge nicht zu viel
Es kommt doch
wie Gott es will.
Do not worry too much
Everything will turn out
As God willed it.
Der treuste Führer in der Not
Das ist und bleibt der liebe Gott.
Zwei Lebenstützen brechen nie
Gebet und Arbeit heissen sie.
The truest leader in times of need
Is and remains beloved God.
Two life supports never fail
Prayer and Work are their names.

If God was the true *Führer*, then who was the false one? Was this text embroidered at the time of Hitler or Ceauşescu? It is only now that this question occurs to me, and I wished that I had asked it at the time.

Frau Kräch opened a factory-made chest of drawers which someone had personalised by painting a traditional flower design and inscribing the date on the top drawer – 1937. Inside, carefully wrapped up in layers of paper and tissue, was a wonderful wardrobe of clothes. She started to dress me in the clothes of an unmarried girl. First, a long white shirt, which was worn under a richly embroidered waistcoat, fastened tight with hooks and eyes. Over a thick white petticoat she gathered a black satin skirt. The fiddliest bits were the decorations – the hairband and choker, the cuffs embellished with separate red ribbons, and the shawl, carefully folded and hung 'just so' over an elaborate apron. Frau Kräch had a large assortment of aprons, each one painstakingly embroidered, and each one differing according to the status of the wearer and the occasion. She scolded as she fussed over my dress. 'No, you have to stand like this,' she said, as she reached up to fasten a pin into my choker. There was a good deal of pulling and prodding involved, as the whole outfit was designed for someone a foot smaller. There were no buttons or zips on these clothes; everything was fastened with ribbons or pins. It recalled to mind and made complete sense of an order from Queen Elizabeth I in the sixteenth century for some 98,000 pins of various sizes for different parts of her dresses, which, judging from the number of pins that went into one Saxon village girl's outfit, no longer seemed excessive.

A true Saxon woman, Frau Kräch would not release me until I was dressed to her complete satisfaction in a style befitting a proper Saxon maiden. My hair had to be tied neatly back without a wisp of it loose, and she was not satisfied until I had made it so. Unmarried girls were

Right: *The Saxons designed their houses to keep themselves and their animals and goods secure behind high gates.*

required to wear an unflattering cylindrical hat covered in velvet with two long embroidered ribbons running down it. She went into a storeroom and pulled out a box of beautifully made hand-crafted boots. In such a traditional community, it was hard to tell how old they were. They could have been either 40 or 80 years old for they had been so carefully made and kept, worn only for church and on festival days, cleaned and brightly polished and stored away in layers of newspaper. Such was the thrift of these people that the boots were made to fit either foot.

Not until Frau Kräch had placed a copy of the *Evangelische Gesangbuch*, the Lutheran hymn-book, and taught me to hold it in the correct way, with both hands, at a diagonal across my lap, did she pronounce with satisfaction, '*Alles in Ordnung; alles in Ordnung*.' Everything was now as it should be. This was Sunday best, for the purpose of worshipping God, and the wardrobe would have been incomplete without the hymn-book, which spoke so much of the Saxon identity in this distant, threatening, exotic land: 'Work and Pray'. In some villages, the Saxons once kept their best clothes

Left: *The pulpit at Meşendorf which has a sand-timer suspended from the gallery at eye level with the pastor to ensure that his sermon does not overrun.*

– the ones that they wore each Sunday and on special occasions – in the church for safe-keeping, carefully returning them on Sunday evening.

Frau Kräch was the only Saxon left in her village to wear traditional clothes to church. She had dressed me in the costume of an unmarried woman; a married woman or a widow would have worn quite different styles. It was almost worth marrying to swap the unflattering black drum hat for the fine white linen headdress of the married woman, tied in such a way as to form a sort of hood like the one in Holbein's portrait of *The Lady with a Squirrel*. Frau Kräch was a widow with four sons. One had died and the others had gone to work in Germany. There were no daughters to dress in the carefully stored clothes, and she lived in her charming house alone.

The immediate effect of wearing the Saxon dress was to make me stand up very straight and conduct myself with decorum. Any temptation to slouch and the hat would have fallen off, or several pins would have come undone and pierced different parts of my body. The house and dress were picturesque, but life as a Saxon – and particularly a Saxon woman in a traditional village – would have been very circumscribed and subject to a strict code of behaviour. Every village had a *Bruderschaft*, or brotherhood, to which all boys belonged from the age of their confirmation until marriage. It was a way of controlling young men at a difficult age and ensuring they conformed to the spirit of the community, upheld its rules and values, and treated others with consideration. *Schwesternschaften*, or sisterhoods, are less well documented. Presumably, they were a less necessary part of village law enforcement since girls' lives were so much more prescribed and they were seen as less of a threat to the equilibrium of the village.

After marriage, a young couple would become members of a *Nachbarschaft* (neighbourhood organisation). Each village was divided into four neighbourhoods presided over by a 'neigbourhood father', who was responsible for ensuring that everyone in his district conducted themselves in an orderly manner. Every aspect of life was regulated in some way – even table manners: 'Anyone who lolls about with his elbows on the table like a Wallach [Romanian] instead of sitting up straight will be fined.' A young man could be fined for being rude to his elders, and anyone who grumbled when a neighbour woke him up in church would also be penalised. It is illuminating that there is no fine for falling asleep, merely for complaining about being woken up. The Saxons were evidently sympathetic to fatigue caused by long sermons and took measures to prevent their pastor from overrunning his allotted time. One or two churches, such as at Meşendorf (Meschendorf), still have the sand clocks positioned by the side of the pulpit, at eye level to the pastor, which ensured that he did not measure his words too carefully.

After the revolution, congregations became so small that everyone now sits together, but previously a person's place in church was a reflection of their status in society. Men and women were segregated, as in an Orthodox church. In most Saxon churches children sat in the choir, with unmarried girls in the front benches, the long embroidered ribbons of their hats trailing down their ramrod-straight backs, and married women behind. Men sat in the the aisles on either side, while young unmarried men were kept at a safe distance in the gallery.

At Biertan, there is a small hut within the fortifications of the church in which quarrelling couples who sought a divorce were locked for a week. They were obliged to share one stool, one knife, one plate, one cup and one bed – the idea being that they should learn to live with each other amicably, learning the benefits of mutual support in a confined space. A regulation ensuring that no girl was left to sit out a dance and that fined a boy for refusing to dance with a girl did not state what would happen if a girl refused a boy. In traditional Romanian society, a girl who refused to dance ran the risk of being ostracised by all the young men in the group and of being insulted by the rhyming couplets the boys used to shout out while they danced.

Different Saxon communities had different punishments. At Viscri, miscreants stood on a 'stone of shame', which everyone passed on their way to church. No aspect of life escaped the watchful eye of the community. There were strict admonitions about the wearing of traditional dress, and any attempt to introduce more fashionable or 'foreign' elements was frowned upon. In Mediaş, records dating back to 1651 warn against all imitation of Hungarian dress, and in the eighteenth century there were attempts to forbid the wearing of any clothes not made in Transylvania. By the start of the nineteenth century, however, Saxons living in towns had abandoned their traditional style of dress and preserved it only for use at confirmation and for celebrations of Saxon culture, such as choirs and dance groups, much as it is used now. In the Saxon villages, the custom lingered for a further 200 years. A mixture of stubborn conservatism and the defiance of an ever-dwindling minority preserved it until the present day. Even in the mid-nineteenth century, the Saxon way of life in the villages was considered anachronistic, a piece of living history recalling past centuries 'of which the present busy generation knows nothing', as one Victorian visitor observed.

At Biertan, a covered wooden stairway leads all the way up the hill to the church, passing through the innermost defence wall and towers. Just as Transylvania offered political freedom to the privileged, so it was a model of religious tolerance. Transylvania, uniquely in Europe, enjoyed a bloodless Reformation, and the new converts to Protestantism came to an equitable arrangement with the Roman Catholics. The Lutheran Saxons and those Hungarians who turned to Calvinism and Unitarianism were all treated as the equals of the Catholic Church, with almost complete freedom of action. All clergymen were given noble status and permitted to attend the Diet. However, the Orthodox Church, to which the majority of ethnic Romanians belonged, was not treated with such enlightened toleration and was simply not recognised.

To the north of the altar at Biertan was the treasure chamber. Empty but for a few old chairs and a Christmas crib, the room's most precious object was now the door itself. It seemed appropriate that this should be so, a sort of parable of the Saxon people. The treasures and the sober, thrifty men and women who hoarded them so carefully had all vanished, but the door remained, still able to exclude the unwanted by means of its extraordinary locking system. This consisted of seven separate mechanisms that, on the turn of one enormous key, all operated simultaneously.

I asked the gatekeeper, who was good-humouredly demonstrating its workings, if there was a bacon tower.

'Yes, it's the one at the bottom of the covered wall by the plum tree,' he replied.

'Is there any bacon in the tower?'

He laughed. 'Not now, a long time ago there was. But not now.'

Nevertheless, I decided to inspect the buildings thoroughly, just in case there was any bacon he had forgotten about. The first tower I came to was a bell tower, and I was able to climb up the ladders into the rafters. I looked down at the three-fold layers of defensive walls, which stood 12 metres high. From this height, they seemed paper-thin although they were, in fact, a metre deep, topped with sloping red tiles like those on the roofs of the village houses below. Looking down on them from above, all the roofs seemed joined together, an undulating

Right: *The Saxon church at Biertan with its many striking towers. Most Saxon churches had a 'Speckturm' or bacon tower, in which the village's supply of ham was kept. Slices would be carefully cut off each week, a tradition that persisted until 1989.*

red carpet dulled by age and dust, stretching out from the church as far as the surrounding hills.

Psalm 80 was a particular favourite of the Saxons: 'Thou hast brought a vine out of Egypt; Thou hast cast out the heathen and planted it. Thou preparedst room before it, and didst cause it to take deep root, and it filled the land. The hills were covered with the shadow of it.' The hills around the village were terraced for the cultivation of vines, although none grow here any more. The same was true of the hops that once grew in this region. Great net boxes still cover many fields, but it is rare to see any hops growing, despite the fact that Romanians produce some excellent beer. The beer manufacturers, most now owned by foreign companies, all use imported hops.

The whole region is dotted with fortified churches. The finest, such as those at Biertan and Sighişoara, have UNESCO World Heritage status, and some have received funding from Germany and even from Britain. There is not enough money to save them all and many are rotting away quietly. I looked down on an orchard within the fortifications, but there was no one left to pick the plums. The ripe fruit lay on the grass where plump flies gorged on it.

***Left:** The few cushions and hymn books on otherwise deserted and dusty pews at Băgaciu (Bogeschdorf), a sign of how few Saxons remain in this village.*

Tombstones of former dignitaries were propped against the inside walls of one of the towers. 'Here lies Christianus Haasz, Pastor.' He died on 16 September 1686, at the age of 54. His beard almost touched the hem of his splendid vestment and paint still picked out his long, delicate eyelashes. The equally fine tomb slab next to him celebrated Brother Bartholomew as 'a light, a noble star, a sturdy pillar of our Saxon home'. The Latin was constructed so that 'our Saxon' formed the centrepiece of the inscription.

The following Sunday, the living version of such a pastor confronted me at the monastery church in Sighişoara. We stood to sing the entrance hymn as he strode up the nave wearing a long black vestment with steely silver clasps, exactly like the ones on the tombstones at Biertan. He was 28 years old, at least half the age of most of his congregation.

I was standing among heavy-framed men and women whose serious church faces were pale as they shook each other by the hand and lilted their 'Grüss Gotts'. The contrast with the Romanian Orthodox church that I had attended the previous week could not have been greater. There, we stood crowded together in smoky intimacy, the mysteries unseen. Here, we kept our distance from each other on orderly pews. In the one church it seemed that we were worshipping a mysterious God, while among the Saxons he was God made man. I could not help feeling that I was in the 'Protestant world of elders', a phrase used by the writer Gregor von Rezzori, who went to school for a time at Braşov during the 1920s. I had entered a world of order, rules and sobriety that I understood all too completely.

The monastery church, so-called because it was once attached to a Dominican monastery, was first recorded in a so-called letter of indulgence of 1298 from Pope Boniface VIII granting 40 days of release from purgatory to all who attended mass there on certain holidays, or who donated or gave in their will money for the church's decoration. During the 1480s, it was transformed into a three-nave *Hallenkirche*, or hall-church, and was rebuilt after a fire in 1676 by Master Veit Gruber from Falkenstein in the Tyrol and Philipp Audring from Salzburg. Craftsmen worked here from all over the German-speaking world. The wood carvings on the altar were made by a Johannes West from Slovakia and the altarpiece by a Slovakian settled in Sibiu. The fine winged altarpiece of 1520 is attributed to Johann Stoss, son of a famous wood-carver, Veit Stoss, from Nuremberg.

The same internationalism, or rather pan-Germanism, was evident in the parish church on the hill, where the

master builder was Jacob Kendlinger von St Wolfgang from Salzburg. Standing at the highest point of the town, the present church was completed, as a charming Latin inscription in the entrance stated, 'with God's help in the year 1488 when, on St Gerard's day, heavy snows broke the fruit trees down'. On my first visit, the church was still closed for restoration, the work of several years funded by the Messerschmitt Foundation, Munich, and the pastor refused to lend me the key. 'It is too dangerous with all the construction work,' he said. At other churches and monuments around Transylvania, I had been cheerfully taken up all sorts of towers with spiral stairs literally worn away, or with floorboards missing at the top of bell towers that stood hundreds of metres above ground. The pastor's refusal seemed to be another example of how the Saxons were always trying to keep others shut out of their lives. Yet the health and safety reasoning behind his refusal also brought me back with

Left: *The neo-classical entrance to the Saxon church of Cincu (Großschenk), founded in the 13th century.*
Right: *Sixteenth-century lock on the door of the sacristy at Richiş (Reichesdorf), a 14th-century church richly decorated with stone carving. The Saxons perfected the art of guarding their possessions and locking out their enemies.*

a jolt to the world that I had left behind. I had been keen to see the restored late fifteenth-century frescoes, which surprisingly had been whitewashed only in 1877, and an inscription at the back of the choir stalls: *'Wer in dys gestül wil stan und nit latyn reden kann, der solt bleyben draus, das ma ym nit mit Kolben laus.'* (He who wants to sit here and cannot speak Latin should stay out, or else be driven out with a stick.)

That Sunday in the monastery church, the stern-looking pastor ascended the swirling baroque pulpit for the sermon. Although he was speaking *hochdeutsch* (German Received Pronunciation) slowly and carefully, it retained a rolling, rural Saxon lilt. Modern German was not his mother tongue, and his own dialect would have been unintelligible to anyone from outside the surrounding area. Born in a village south of Sighişoara, he had completed his education, in the tradition of countless generations of Saxon clergymen, in Austria and Germany. He could have stayed abroad but had felt a moral obligation to return: 'The old people need the church. It is the focal point of their lives. There are so few young people here now.'

Hanging from church walls and over the side of pews were more than 30 oriental carpets. They looked extremely odd, these gorgeous oriental rugs in a Protestant church, and introduced a hint of exoticism

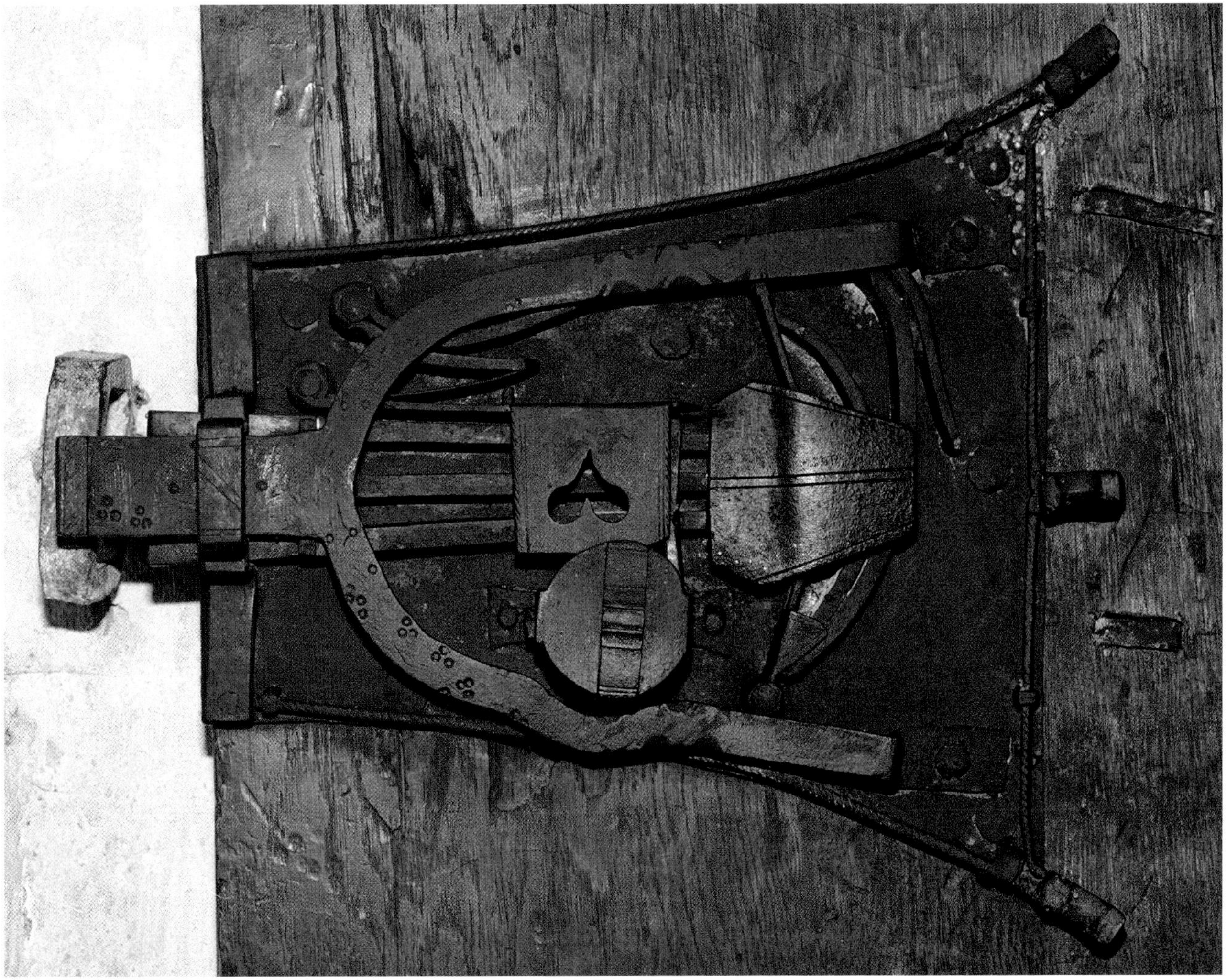

into this practical Lutheran world. It was a reminder of how different this country was to Germany and to other parts of Europe, however much the Saxons had tried to make it otherwise. Such carpets hung in other Saxon churches, too, most famously in the great Black Church in Braşov and in the splendid fortified church at Mediaş, both sizeable towns. About 380 rugs remain in the property of the Transylvanian churches, and from dedications written on the back of them, it is clear that some rugs have hung in the same church for up to 350 years.

The presence of oriental carpets hanging in Protestant churches is often seen as puzzling or mysterious. It has been suggested that they were put there after the Reformation to brighten up interiors which had lost their wall paintings to limewash. One explanation for their almost miraculous survival in a country otherwise despoiled of so many of its treasures is because the church authorities guarded them so zealously. By contrast, rugs in private collections, such as those of the seventeenth-century Transylvanian Prince Gabriel Bethlen, who owned more than 250 oriental carpets, have not withstood the various tribulations that have befallen this region and have been lost or dispersed abroad.

Left: *Seventeenth-century Turkish white-ground Selendi 'bird' rug hanging on the walls of the fortified Saxon church of St Margaret, in the centre of Mediaş.*

Long before the Reformation, rugs were part of the furniture of churches throughout Europe. Although they have long since disappeared elsewhere, their presence is attested in paintings. *The Mass of Saint Giles*, in the National Gallery, London, shows the interior of the Abbey of Saint-Denis near Paris in about 1500, with a carpet prominently displayed in front of the altar and a smaller one covering a small table to one side. The Saxon churches also owned rugs long before the Reformation. In medieval times, rugs were symbols of high status and wealth; they were hung on walls, used to cover tables, and displayed on balconies like celebratory flags. A watercolour of a lost wall painting from Cowdray House in Sussex vividly depicts merchants hanging out carpets and tapestries from the windows of their houses when King Edward VI passed through the City of London in his coronation procession in 1547. It made perfect sense for the Saxons to decorate their churches with some of their most valuable possessions, as a way both of honouring their church and of displaying their personal wealth in public. Everyone had their appointed place in church, and carpets marked the position of the most important personages, such as the seats of the guild members in towns. The habit of displaying carpets in church long after they ceased to have the same status in the West and were no longer used for decorative purposes on walls or tables is also perfectly in keeping with the Saxon conservatism and tendency to hoard possessions.

Dedications on the back of rugs and surviving wills suggest that most came into the possession of the churches as the gift of parishioners or guilds or legacies. Documents also show that the most important Saxon cities owned large numbers of rugs, which they either bought with money from customs dues or were given in the place of customs. These rugs became the property of the town and were used as gifts to important dignitaries, as part of tribute to the Turks or as payment in kind.

Saxon merchants continued to buy and trade Turkish rugs up to the end of the eighteenth century, but by then interest in them had waned. As elsewhere in Europe, the fashion was for carpets made to western taste in French or Viennese factories. There is some indication, however, that the carpets were not always exhibited as they are now and that the habit of displaying them in church also fell out of fashion. Nineteenth-century travel writers, otherwise keen observers of Saxon traditions, make surprisingly little mention of them. Auguste de Gérando, writing in the mid-1840s, is silent on the subject. Charles Boner, visiting Braşov's Black Church, which now houses one of the most remarkable collections of carpets in Transylvania, enthuses about some precious old vestments he sees in the vestry in 1863 and frets about their worrying state of preservation, but makes no mention of seeing any carpets. Emily Gerard, usually so discursive, refers dismissively to the moth-eaten carpets 'brought back from Turkish campaigns' that she sees hung over the back of the organ gallery and pews in some village churches.

In Mediaş in about 1900, a pile of rugs was discovered in the vestry, and there is a record that women selected those in a good state of repair and covered the pews with them. It is possible that, having lost their status in the eighteenth century, the carpets were carefully stored away until an interest sparked by the Arts and Crafts movement in the late nineteenth century provided the impetus to display them once more. Some were also cut in half to cover church benches and seat backs.

In the first decades of the twentieth century, there was something of a rug-hunting craze. Many Protestant Hungarian churches, some of which had modest collections of rugs, sold them off at this time. An anecdote quoted in Stefano Ionescu's *Antique Ottoman Rugs in Transylvania* reports the experiences of a collector who acquired a carpet in 1935. It had a section missing because the previous winter someone had cut off it off to wrap around his leg for warmth.

That the Saxon churches own such a huge number of rugs is testament to their astonishing tenacity and care. Fortunately, by the time of the Second World War, the value of the rugs was fully recognised and some of the most important collections were moved to safety. The church at Bistriţa moved 57 rugs to Germany during the war, and later stored them in Nuremberg.

Back in von Rezzori's 'Protestant world of elders', the pastor was still preaching, and I had long ago lost track of what he was saying. I looked through the hymn-book. Martin Luther's great hymn of the Reformation, '*Ein' feste Burg ist unser Gott*' (A strong fortress is our God), might have been written for the Transylvanian Saxons, so clearly did it state their physical and spiritual relationship with God. There was a whole section at the back of the hymn-book devoted to *Arbeit, Beruf, Vaterland* (Work, Occupation, Fatherland). On the north side of the wall separating the nave from the chancel was a memorial to those who had lost their lives in two World Wars and in the deportations to Russia in 1947. Such memorials are always sad, but when they are dedicated to young soldiers who were officially one's enemies yet express the same sentiments of grief, loss and praise – 'Our Dead Heroes', 'They Died that We Might Live' – war seems doubly futile.

An especially poignant characteristic of memorials in the Saxon villages is that, in addition to the names of the dead and the dates of their birth and death, they also list the number of the house at which each person lived. This small detail broadens the sense of loss beyond the individual to each family and street. For a moment, the people come briefly to life once more and inhabit the houses standing in the street outside.

During the First World War, Transylvania was still part of the Austro-Hungarian Empire and fought on the German side, while Romania, with an English queen and a German king on the throne, procrastinated before joining the Allies in 1916. Their prize at the end of the war was an enlarged Romania incorporating Transylvania. In the Second World War, however, after two years' uneasy neutrality, in 1941 Romania joined the war on the side of the Germans. In June 1940, while Romania sat in an increasingly precarious state of neutrality, the Germans forced it to cede northern Transylvania to their Hungarian allies. The Romanian government concluded an agreement with the Germans in 1943, whereby young ethnic Germans in Romania could be drafted into the German Army to serve, in particular, in the Waffen-SS. The division of Transylvania meant that during the course of the war Saxons served in the Romanian, Hungarian or German armies, depending on their age and whether they lived in

northern or southern Transylvania. When Romania switched sides in August 1944 as the Red Army was fast approaching its borders, the Saxons found themselves in a difficult position. By autumn 1944, the Russians had 'liberated' Bucharest and helped the Romanians drive Hungarian and German forces out of Transylvania, occupying Sibiu by September.

After the war, 70,000 ethnic Germans were accused of collaboration with the Nazis and sentenced to hard labour in the Soviet Union for between one and four years. Men between the ages of 17 and 45 and women between 18 and 30 were deported. Those who survived found on their return that the Communists had confiscated their land and divided their property. They found their spacious houses split in two or three and were ordered to share their accommodation with Romanian families. The Romanian Communist Party in one fell swoop snatched land that the Saxons had held onto for centuries against all threat from the Turks, Tatars, Austrians and Hungarians. It was a bitter blow. That this also happened to a large number of Romanians seems, however, not to have registered among the elderly Saxon community.

Left: *Commemoration of the life of Michael Wagner of Viscri, war veteran, who in old age wrote several accounts of life in a Saxon village.*

Left: *The great fourteenth-century clocktower at Sighişoara, once the main entrance into the fortified town.*
Right: *Snowy rooftops in the medieval centre of Sighişoara.*

When I asked 100-year-old Herr Dootz whether he thought of himself as Saxon, German or Romanian, he looked at me in astonishment, as though I had asked a question so stupid that he could barely understand it. 'I am Saxon and a German. The two are absolutely one and the same thing.' Only the very few members of the younger generation, such as 20-year-old Johann Schaaser, who had grown up in the Saxon village of Saschiz (Keisd) where the concept of a Saxon community had already disappeared before he was old enough to appreciate the loss, thought of themselves as both Saxon and Romanian. An old Saxon man in Sighişoara summed up his people's history in the second half of the twentieth century like this: 'Our hands were tied, then our lips were sealed.'

Two old women I met outside the monastery church in Sighişoara one Sunday morning had been transported to Russia in their late teens. One of them had been released after a year, apparently because the doctor had said that she was too small and weak; the other, who was called Margarethe, had endured four years in the coal mines. 'They moved us round all the time in the camps, so we never made friends,' she said. 'And we had so little to eat. We had to work so hard for one potato.'

Johann Dootz had been more fortunate. As a builder, he had a useful skill and the Russians had ordered him to construct a factory, telling him that he could return home when he had finished it. That was in spring and he had been determined to build it before the snows came in winter, so that he could return to Transylvania. To the amazement of the Russians, he managed to complete it, and they kept their word and let him return.

After the church service, I stayed behind to copy out a hymn that seemed like a particularly good example of the Saxon mentality and struck up a conversation with a Saxon man in his sixties who was one of the church stewards. He said: 'We work with our hands and survive with our heads. And we pray. That is the philosophy of the Saxon people.' He suggested that if I wished to know about Saxon culture, then I should talk to Professor Hermann Beier, choir master and mathematics teacher at the German school on the hill, and it was Professor Beier who told me where to find the ham.

He agreed to meet after choir practice on Monday evening. The rehearsal took place at the culture hall next door to the great clock tower, and German songs were ringing out from the windows across the square as I approached. The clock tower, once the main entrance gate into the citadel, dates from the fourteenth century and stands 64 metres tall. It now houses a museum of town history, with small exhibitions on each floor. One display features Hermann Oberth, one of the 'founding fathers of space travel', who was born in the town. He worked in Germany during the Second World War developing, among other things, the devastating V2-rockets, and then worked on the space rocket programme in America during the 1950s. Right at the top of the tower, above the elaborate seventeenth-century clock mechanism and the painted gods that depict each day of the week (Wednesday is Mercury and on Friday Venus appears), was an open gallery. On its ledges were metal plates with the names of cities written on them and arrows pointing in the direction in which they lay and their distance in kilometres: Prague, Belgrade, London and New York were there, but most were German towns. During the years when their hands were tied and their lips were sealed, did the citizens of Sighişoara come up here to dream of all the places they might escape to when they were free? If Ceauşescu had ever climbed up there, would he have had them removed?

'They are just amateurs. I am an amateur,' Professor Beier said after the choir practice, as we leafed through his choral music in a nearby café: traditional Saxon songs, Beethoven, Elgar and Bach, and a few Romanian songs. 'I have to admit more and more Romanians into the choir to keep up the numbers. In Communist times we always had to have a percentage of Romanians but now there are a lot more.' Without the Romanians, the 40-strong choir would have been a fraction of its size.

Saxon food had apparently borrowed from Romanian and Hungarian recipes, so it was more piquant than food in Germany, but to my disappointment the restaurant where we met sold only pizzas and grilled meat. The traditional village recipes were no longer made or the knowledge had been taken to Germany. Professor Beier had not eaten *Hanklich* for a long time. This was often mentioned as a particular Saxon treat, a cross between bread and cake, made flat in a square tin with flour, yeast, butter, milk, eggs and sugar. It was eaten, with cream spread on top, at special celebrations. And what about the bacon?

'Yes, we used to keep our ham in the bacon towers. Each family had a numbered space to hang their bacon in the tower, and every week, either before or after church or sometimes on Saturday night, depending on the custom of the village, we went to cut off slices for the following week.'

'Do you know anyone who still keeps bacon in a bacon tower?'

'Not now,' he said. 'There is no one left to eat it.' Then he recalled that the previous spring he had seen some hanging in a village about 16 kilometres south of Sighişoara. 'I think the family must have forgotten about it,' he said, 'and left it hanging there when they went to Germany.'

I could not wait to go there. The countryside rolled and the road wrapped round it, but it still did not look like England. The fields had no hedges or walls, and groups of gypsies milled outside the crumbling Saxon houses. Bundles of children played in the road. The church stood on a hill at a crossroads, surrounded by a thick wall and high gate covered in dense vegetation. Like Sleeping Beauty's castle when the thorns had surrounded it, nettles, weeds and creeping plants everywhere choked the crumbling walls. Only a chicken wire frame blocked the church porch to prevent the sheep from climbing in. The day was overcast, which made the deep grass look black and the towers despondent in their decay.

Sparrows swooped in and out of the church. The walls were painted white, so it was surprisingly much brighter inside than out. It was very plain. I walked up into the gallery, and the benches there were covered in years of dust. Only four narrow benches nearest the altar had cushions on them, for the few Saxons who had come to the last service here a month previously.

Right: *The bell-tower at Băgaciu, with the old Saxon school in the foreground. The church was besieged by the Turks in 1661 and the village burned.*

On leaving the church, the floor of the first tower contained grave-digging equipment, but even that was rusty and covered in dust. Sheep droppings covered the floor of the next tower. The beams had numbers incised on them in elegant Gothic script, corresponding to the number of each house, so that everyone knew which bacon was theirs. With typical Saxon thoroughness, it was also the custom to stamp the bottom of the bacon after cutting the weekly slices, to ensure that no one was tempted to creep in and steal from the family ham during the rest of the week. All that remained, however, was a hook with a taunting piece of knotted string wrapped round the beam.

Six yellow eyes stared out of the pitch dark, as if suspended in the blackness. As my sight gradually adjusted, I saw three sheep huddled against the back wall, and I advanced towards the centre of the room. In between them and me, hanging from the central beam like a boxer's punch bag, was an enormous side of bacon so thick with dust and grime that I could not work out how decayed it was. Next to it were one and a half sides of ham. A scrap of newspaper was wrapped round the rafter above them and I pulled it down. Covered in damp globules of dust was a photograph of Elena and Nicolae Ceauşescu in Yugoslavia, there to lay a wreath on Tito's grave. Tito died in 1980, so it must postdate that. Perhaps the family who left the ham behind had managed to go to Germany before the revolution, forced to leave everything behind, including their bacon.

I walked down the hill and round the back of the mound on which the fortification was raised, behind a gaggle of geese waddling through the mud. There were some impoverished-looking houses on either side of the lane and a wrought-iron well in the middle of it. Just beyond, a covered wooden staircase led up a hill to a pretty, whitewashed church. On either side of the stairway, well-tended graves grew out of the long grass. The Romanian Orthodox church, unencumbered by defensive walls, gently reflected the pale pink afternoon light.

Looking towards the Saxon church, I thought how strange the pre-war bacon anecdote was. It did not ring true. Such thrifty people would never have left a perfectly good ham go to waste just because there had been no siege, however obsessed with hoarding they were. They would have come and carefully cut off a slice of meat and pork fat every week after church and eked out the supply until they slaughtered the next pig. Even the newspaper found in the rafters was not left there out of carelessness. It was used to wrap up the bacon slices. A Saxon would only leave a ham if forced to leave his home.

The Saxons had given up on Transylvania. They had gone back to the place from which they came, their *Urheimat*, for exactly the same reasons that they had first left 800 years earlier. It was the promise of greater economic and political freedom that made them abandon their bacon. Pity the Saxons that they felt the need to go. Pity Romania that they have left.

Right: *The stages of man, a nineteenth-century print mended over the decades by its careful Saxon owners. Note the handwritten inscription for man's 50th year. It was one of the very few possessions to survive two World Wars and the deportations to Russia. When its owner returned from Siberia, he found his house divided into two under the Communists and occupied by another family, but the print was still hanging on the wall.*

DAS STUFENALTER DES MANNES.

Left: Bran Castle and the surrounding countryside. Its links to Dracula are somewhat tenuous. Connections are closer with Queen Victoria's granddaughter, Queen Marie of Romania.

Chapter 2

An Imaginative Whirlpool

The fictional character that has cast the longest shadow over western perceptions of Transylvania – and Romania – is Dracula. Even now, the vocabulary of a gothic novel is often used whenever Romania is discussed, with those stories that best conform to the stereotypical image of a quaint land inhabited by vampires making the news. Orphanages, pollution, corruption, immigration – all make good horror stories, especially when a few references to Dracula are included.

Four centuries before Bram Stoker invented the vampire Count Dracula in 1897, the whole of Europe was entertained to gruesome accounts of the misdeeds of the Wallachian Prince Vlad III Dracula, a creature of legendary cruelty even in his own lifetime. In an era where torture, execution and violent death were commonplace, the prince's monstrous behaviour was outstanding in its ghastliness and managed to shock and titillate the known world. Thanks to the recent invention of the printing press, his enemies – the Saxons of Transylvania – were able to distribute sensational pamphlets with titles such as 'About the Vile Tyrant, Voivode Dracul' and 'An Extraordinary and Shocking History of a Great Tyrant Called Draculea Voda', illustrated with crude woodcuts showing his victims being impaled and tortured. These proved so popular that they continued to be printed decades after his death. Two manuscripts relating his cruelties, the so-called *German Tales*, written in a Low German dialect, survive from as early as 1462, at the time of Dracula's imprisonment in Budapest, as well as a poem by Michael Beheim entitled *About a Brute Called Trakle, Voivode of Wallachia*. Official reports of his deeds also found their way to the Vatican, Constantinople and Moscow.

One of the problems about any discussion of Dracula today is that he is in fact three or four different characters. Even when considering the 'historical' Dracula as opposed to Bram Stoker's vampiric version, one needs to bear in mind that this fifteenth-century prince has undergone many attempts to exaggerate his deeds and character – both to blacken his name and also to eulogise it.

His name alone can be confusing. Although the historical prince signed some surviving documents as Dracula and was known by this name to the Saxons, the Romanians called him Vlad Ţepeş. 'Ţepeş' is the Romanian for impaler, and he was given this nickname because of his notorious method of punishing his enemies. In Romania, he was regarded as a great national hero. In order to simplify matters, he will be referred to only as Dracula from now on.

There have been various suggestions as to why the Saxons hated Dracula so much and speculation as to the true extent of his cruelty. In the poem of Michael Beheim, he is a monstrous tyrant who inflicted pain on the scale of Herod, Diocletian and Nero. Some of the fifteenth-century pamphlets printed after his death present the story of Dracula as a moral tale. It was only after the Orthodox prince converted to Catholicism while imprisoned by the Hungarian king that he ceased his evil ways: 'They say Dracula only does very good works now that he has become a Christian.'

During Dracula's lifetime, there is vivid evidence from surviving letters in the Saxon archives and from other contemporary reports of the continually shifting relationship between Dracula and the Saxons. Some letters from him are friendly, such as those in which he agrees to provide assistance against the Turks and other enemies or to let the merchants of Braşov trade freely in Wallachia. In others he issues threats and complaints, protesting against the Saxons sheltering a pretender to the Wallachian throne. In one letter he is keen to reassure the Saxons that despite Turkish requests to pass through Wallachia on their way to attack Transylvania, he will not allow it. In another he accuses the citizens of Sibiu of stirring up trouble and threatens them with reprisals.

Each party had to bear in mind which side was most likely to win, whose star was in the ascendant. Were the Turks going to be a threat this year? Was the pretender to the Wallachian throne likely to receive support from Hungarian interests instead of Dracula? Which Hungarian prince was likely to back which side? The Saxons' primary interests were in trade and in securing their economic and political privileges. They supported any leader who was likely to cause least disruption to their finances. Several of the German horror stories were connected with trade disputes, relating how Saxon merchants from Braşov had their goods confiscated and were impaled. Yet the Saxons were nothing if not pragmatists, and despite claims that Dracula killed and tortured tens of thousands of Saxons in his lifetime – figures which must be exaggerations, on grounds of population alone – they continued to offer him shelter in Transylvania throughout his life.

Dracula's notoriety lived on for some time after his death in battle in 1476. But, over the centuries, his memory among the German-speaking peoples fell into near oblivion, perpetuated only in the occasional history of the region. After the sixteenth century, his name was celebrated only in the odd Romanian folk-tale and by anyone who visited the Cabinet of Curiosities of Ferdinand II, Archduke of Tyrol. Here Dracula's portrait

***Right:** Funeral feast in Maramureş. Men and women are segregated, as they are in church.*

can still be found among the other villains and freaks which the archduke had pleasure in collecting, occasionally in the flesh, for the delectation of his court. Dracula died long before the archduke acquired his portrait at the second half of the sixteenth century. It is possible that the painting is a copy of one taken from life while Dracula was imprisoned in Budapest; there is also a miniature in Vienna, now in the Kunsthistorisches Museum. It certainly bears a fair likeness to an account written by the Croatian Bishop Niccolò Modrussiense, who as papal legate of Pope Pius II attended King Matthias Corvinus's court in Buda between 1463 and 1464 and met Dracula while he was there:

'He was not very tall, but he had a strong, healthy body and a savage, frightening countenance, with a large aquiline nose, flared nostrils, and a thin, reddish face. Large grey-green eyes stared out from under heavy eyelids. They were framed by bushy black eyebrows which made them seem menacing. His face and chin were clean-shaven apart from a moustache. Swollen temples increased the bulk of his head. His bull-like neck stood on broad shoulders and curly dark-brown hair fell down onto them.'

Left: *Looking towards the tailors' tower, one of nine surviving towers (out of 14) in Sighişoara. The guilds were responsible for the construction, maintenance and defence of the towers.*

The only differences between this literary portrait and the paintings in Austria are that Dracula's eyebrows are much more elegantly shaped in the paintings and are not in the least bushy.

Dracula's fame as a historical figure was only resurrected in the nineteenth century by nationalists keen to find heroes to galvanise a fledgling Romanian nation. As early as 1853, Dracula was transformed from a crazed, evil tyrant into a great military leader, a champion of the poor and defender of law and order. The Communists took up this version of Dracula with enthusiasm. Romanians, especially during Ceauşescu's time, were brought up to revere the historical Prince Vlad as a national hero who fought terrific battles against the Turks. He was presented as a brave and just ruler who would not tolerate any sort of dishonesty or theft and who would deal harshly with those who broke his laws. Anyone who threatened the stability of his country, or did not respect its customs, was also punished. The Turkish envoys who refused to remove their turbans in Dracula's presence 'because it was not their custom' had them nailed to their heads.

While the Communists glorified him as a great defender of his country's independence against the Turks, he really only played a bit part in the struggle with the Ottomans, although he seems to have fought them fiercely, if not to say savagely, and won some short-lived victories. Wallachia and Moldavia were not subject to Turkish rule in the same way as the Serbian and Bulgarian lands because the two principalities were not on the main route into Western Europe. The road went from Belgrade via the Hungarian capital of Buda to Vienna, so there was no necessity to travel through Romanian territory. It was thus far more profitable to the Turks to give the principalities some small autonomy and bind them to pay enormous amounts of tribute for the privilege.

The Turks were also a constant threat to Transylvania during the fifteenth century. They were kept at bay by the Transylvanian Prince John Hunyadi, who managed to defeat them twice on Transylvanian soil in 1441–3, and as regent of Hungary he gained a resounding victory against them at Belgrade in 1456. But in 1526, Sultan Suleiman the Magnificent inflicted his devastating defeat on the Hungarians at the battle of Mohács, which marked the beginning of the end for Hungary as an independent kingdom. From 1541, when the Turks occupied Buda, Transylvania became a semi-autonomous principality under Turkish suzerainty. For one fleeting year before his murder in 1601, the Wallachian King Michael the Brave, known in Romanian as Mihai Viteazul, united the three principalities of Transylvania, Wallachia and Moldavia under his rule. For Romanian nationalists in the nineteenth century and later the Communists, Michael the Brave was seized upon as an iconic figure who symbolised the struggle for national unity, just as Dracula was elevated as a champion of national freedom against the Turks and a just ruler (if an insanely harsh one) who exacted absolute honesty from his subjects. It was not until the Polish King John Sobieski drove back the Turks from the gates of Vienna in 1683 that Ottoman influence in the region declined and Austro-Hungary became the dominant force.

The Dracula legend has been further complicated in the past few decades by a desire by Romania's tourism industry to exploit the world's fascination with him. This tourist Dracula cheerfully conflates every possible version of him in existence – fact and fiction, demon and hero – and invites the visitor to a number of locations, some connected with the historical Dracula, some with Stoker's creation. Others, such as Bran Castle, have no discernible links with either character at all. So, at Târgovişte, the former capital of Wallachia, are the ruins of the historical Dracula's palace. Snagov Monastery, near Bucharest, is his alleged burial place. In Bram Stoker's novel, Jonathan Harker travels through the Borgo Pass to the fictional Dracula's castle, a dark, brooding, semi-ruinous place. Today, 'Dracula Castle' stands at the highest point on the tortuous pass, a kitsch modern hotel surrounded by tacky souvenir shops and tourist coaches.

The fortified town of Sighişoara would provide a perfect setting to illustrate a book of children's fairy-tales. Viewing the old citadel from across the river or approaching it from the modern town below, it looks like those depictions of ethereal cities that are often found painted very small in the corner of medieval paintings, with towers and church spires rising above their perfectly circular, paper-thin walls. Sighişoara's defensive walls look impossibly thin; its towers and spires rise up in layers, with the Gothic church on the hill its pinnacle. Nine of the original fourteen towers and two out of five bastions survive along the defensive wall, which dates from the fourteenth century. Each tower is still known by the name of the guild that sponsored its building and defence, such as the goldsmiths' tower, the ironworkers' tower and the leatherworkers' tower. The tailors' tower, next to the pastor's house on the way up to the church on the hill, would make an ideal model for Rapunzel's prison. What is more difficult to imagine in this picturesque and obviously German old quarter is the fact that Dracula – the 'real' Dracula – was born here.

On entering the old town underneath the monumental fourteenth-century clock tower, where Professor Beier held his choir rehearsals, a row of prosperous merchants' houses face the monastery church. One of these sturdy houses, painted bright ochre, has a sign in the shape of a cartoon Dracula outside it. In spite of the fact that it has fangs, and blood trickling from the sides of its mouth, the character looks jovial – as well it might, as it is there to entice passers-by to visit the Dracula restaurant. Those who enter of their own free will may well be met by a waiter in a long cloak, possibly sporting plastic fangs. Considering the tacky lengths to which the proprietors could have gone, however, the interior is quite restrained. In spite of the odd wrought-iron bat on the wall, it retains an atmosphere of having belonged for many centuries to respectable Saxon citizens.

A plaque on the exterior, reassuring by its sober presence, states that Vlad Dracul, ruler of the Romanian lands and son of Mircea the Old, lived in this house during the years 1431–5. It is not clear exactly what evidence there is to link the family so closely with this particular house. It appears that a building on or near this spot was used as an official guesthouse. As the Saxons of Sighişoara were giving shelter to Dracula's father Vlad Dracul, a Wallachian prince who was seeking his country's throne at the time of Dracula's birth in about 1431, it is assumed that the foreign prince's family would have stayed in the official residence and that Dracula would have been born here. But it is still hard to imagine that one of the most notoriously cruel rulers in history was born among Saxon merchants in the heart of one of their greatest fortified towns.

Also around 1431, Sigismund of Luxembourg, King of Hungary and Holy Roman Emperor, invested Dracula's father with the Order of the Dragon. Established to fight the Turks, this order obliged all those who belonged to it to wear insignia with the sign of the dragon and a cross. Vlad Dracul had a dragon flag, and before his accession to the throne in 1436, he minted coins in Sighişoara depicting a dragon on one side. The Latin for dragon is *draco*, which also means a snake or serpent. In Romanian, the definite article is put after the noun, so *dracul* means 'the dragon'.

One of the curiosities about the name is that in Romanian *drac* also means devil, and there has been some debate as to whether the princes, because of their

Right: *Vlad Tepeş 'Dracula' was supposedly born in Sighişoara's official guesthouse, which stood on the site of the Saxon house (facing).*

evil deeds, were called Dracula through associations with the Devil. Did the people of those times, seeing the dragon standard, associate the image and the person carrying it with the Devil? The Romanian words for dragon and devil are identical, but any Orthodox, God-fearing Wallachian would also be familiar with the imagery of the dragon in a Christian context. Often found on top of the iconostasis in an Orthodox church are two dragons, their heads turned behind them and their tails curled round their heads. All would know that this was a symbol of the triumph of good over evil and was no satanic sign, especially as the Order of the Dragon also bore the sign of the Cross.

William Wilkinson wrote of his experiences as British consul in Bucharest in 1820, some 50 years before Romania became a nation state and long before either the creation of the fictional vampire Count Dracula or the elevation of Vlad Dracula into a national hero. In his account, he notes, 'Dracula in the Wallachian language means Devil. The Wallachians were, at that time, as they are at present, used to give this as a surname to any person who rendered himself conspicuous either by courage, cruel actions or cunning.'

A medieval German chronicler certainly used Dracula's name with terrifying simplicity in his account of an attack on the area around Amnaş (Hamlesch), near Sibiu. On St Bartholomew's Day 1460, he reports: '*des morgens ist der Dracoll komen uber der waldt mit sinen dienern*' (in the morning Dracula came over the forest with his servants). This makes it sound as though Dracula flew over the trees like the Devil himself, with winged demons in attendance.

Although Bran Castle, near Braşov, in Transylvania, has the most tenuous – not to say nonexistent – links with Dracula, it too has become a feature of the Dracula trail and one of the most visited attractions in Romania, often marketed as 'Castle Dracula'. Yet, Bran Castle no more captures a sense of Dracula fact or fiction than does the delightful old centre of Sighişoara. Founded in the thirteenth century by the Teutonic Knights, it was later under the control of the Saxon citizens of nearby Braşov, and was a strategic site guarding one of the two main passes between Transylvania and Wallachia.

The castle was entirely rebuilt by Queen Victoria's granddaughter, Queen Marie of Romania, and was decorated and furnished in her eclectic taste during the 1920s. It became the summer residence of the Romanian royal family, with rooms furnished in a mixture of Art Deco, traditional Romanian and German baronial styles. The story is told that in the early 1980s, in order to make the place more frightening so that it lived up to the expectations of tourists visiting it on the premise that it had connections with Dracula, employees used to hide in chests and leap out at visitors. The trick is said to have worked so well that one American suffered a heart attack. Since then the practice has stopped.

It is surprising that the castle of Hunedoara is not presented as a Dracula attraction, as it has an infinitely gloomier atmosphere than Bran and its founder, Prince John Hunyadi, the great fifteenth-century Transylvanian warrior against the Turks, and his son played leading roles in the fate of Dracula's family. As Hunyadi came from a Romanian aristocratic family that had been assimilated into the Hungarian nobility, the Romanians claim him as their own and call him Ioan or Iancu Hunedoara. But he was a Catholic Hungarian nobleman who was responsible for the death of Dracula's father and brother, according to some sources, including the contemporary *Commentaries* of Pope Pius II.

Right: *Bran Castle guarded one of the main passes between Transylvania and Wallachia.*
Previous page, left: *During the service on All Souls' Day, when all the dead of the village are commemorated, the priest blesses offerings of bread, illuminated with candles.*
Previous page, right: *On the eve of All Souls' Day, women tend the family graves and light candles.*

Hunyadi's son, Matthias Corvinus, became one of Hungary's most celebrated kings, much influenced by Italian Renaissance culture; he added many graceful decorative elements to his father's splendid late Gothic castle. The Vajdahunyad Castle in the City Park in Budapest, built to celebrate 1,000 years of Hungarian history in 1896, is in part a copy of Hunyadi's castle in Transylvania. Originally built in wood and cardboard as a temporary structure for the festivities, it was subsequently erected permanently and shows a mixture of architectural styles, including – rather bizarrely – a copy of the Saxon clock tower in Sighişoara. It was Corvinus who imprisoned Dracula in Hungary for 12 years, purportedly for offering to betray Transylvania to the Turks, and a number of people who met him in Buda at the time have recorded their impressions of him, including Niccolò Modrussiense, whose devastating description of Dracula is mentioned above. Although a prisoner, he was not kept in a dank dungeon, but accorded the privileges due to him as a prince.

Built on a rock high above the modern town, Hunedoara Castle now glowers over what was once one of the largest centres of iron and steel production in Romania. From the outside, the castle has enormous dramatic impact, and the view from the battlements – looking out over the skeletal remains of the steel production plants and giant industrial chimneys which seem to stand eye to eye with Hunedoara's towers – would provide a perfect backdrop for a postmodern Gothic fantasy with Dracula in the starring role.

The castle was destroyed by fire in the 1850s and then suffered from decades of neglect. This was followed by over-enthusiastic restoration programmes in the nineteenth and early twentieth centuries, in which architects projected onto it their own wistful interpretations of how a great Gothic castle should look. The same sense of fantasy continues today, with props from a film recently shot there left 'to add atmosphere', as a guide at the castle related.

The Hungarian traveller Auguste de Gérando despaired when he saw the castle even before it was badly damaged by fire:

The work of Matthias Corvinus is unrecognisable … vaulting is cut up by new walls and Gothic windows have been enlarged in a most bourgeois way. One cannot visit this castle without cursing the parsimony of the Austrian government which does not have a few thousand florins to

Left: *Hunedoara Castle, the much destroyed and restored Gothic castle founded in the 15th century by John Hunyadi, the great warrior prince against the Turks.*

construct its offices elsewhere ... the modern rooms formed out of I don't know what combination are mostly dark and incommodious. They lack even the miserable regularity of administrative offices. Thus has a national monument been ruined for so little!

The place that most closely recalled the feeling of vulnerability and terror which Dracula's name – indeed any potential enemy, whether Vlach, Turk or Tatar – evoked among the Saxons was not in a castle but in the obscure village of Bonnersdorf, now called Boian. We arrived there one evening in May, just as the light was fading. The closer we drove to the village, the more potholed the road became and the more flat and desolate the landscape. Boian's one street was a mud track with a long line of houses on either side. They were all built in the traditional Saxon style but were rundown, with peeling paint and patched up roofs and windows. Despite their neglected appearance and the obvious poverty of the place, many people were on the street, which added life to an otherwise sombre scene. Most of the villagers were standing in small groups or sitting outside their houses. One man stood, hands in pocket, leaning against

***Left:** The crumbling fifteenth-century fortified church at Boian (Bonnersdorf).*

the only shop window in the village, and a few young men were experiencing that strange magnetic pull that teenagers everywhere have towards bus stops. A sense of expectation hung in the air, as it does in every Romanian village just before the cows come home.

The night was drawing in rapidly, the day's work in the fields was done, and these were the last moments to run an errand or chat to a neighbour before the evening retreat behind gates to feed animals and family and retire to bed. My anticipation was of a different kind – an excitement at visiting a fortified church that I had never seen before, mingled with the anxiety that the light would soon begin to fail. We had to find the church keyholder and persuade him to turn out at this crucial time in the evening.

The usual key-searching scenario unfolded. We approached an old woman sitting on a bench outside her house, eager to catch the very last gossip of the day, to see if she could help us. We had to repeat this several times. Maybe it was our strange accents or perhaps she was deaf, but by the time she acknowledged that she understood our message, a bunch of grinning children in grimy tracksuits and rubber boots surrounded us, and it now seemed as though everyone in the village knew our business. Even so, the old woman felt it necessary to shout to a neighbour who called to a child, and a whole new crowd of smiling excited boys and girls in ancient hand-me-downs were at our side. Their mud-stained clothes and faces were the evidence of lives spent largely out of doors, running errands for their parents in the fields, helping with the chickens and cows at home, and playing in the streets with their friends. About five anxious minutes later, the children returned, escorting two old men in straw hats dark with decades of labour. They both walked very slowly. The keyholder, Herr Wagner, and his friend represented two-fifths of the Saxon population of Boian. They told us that the other three members of the community were the same age as themselves – in their mid-seventies – or older.

The church sat at the top of the main street behind a ring wall four metres tall. Properly fortified with two great towers, the barrel-vaulted main entrance under the gate tower clearly once had a portcullis, and around the interior of the defensive wall a partial two-storey walkway ran between the battlements. Everything was crumbling and we stood calf-deep in weeds, but there was something about this place that suited neglect. Perhaps the collective expectancy of nightfall and the running clouds of a damp, inclement May day all contributed to the brooding atmosphere, but it certainly had an extraordinary feel to it, a sense of lingering disaster, as though it had been party to gloomy and frightening moments in history.

Adding to the sense of strangeness was the sight of the arms of King Stephen the Great of Moldavia, Dracula's cousin, on the outside wall of the bell tower and then again over the north door. The golden aurochs, or bison, with a crescent moon and star between its horns was a symbol of another world; a more Byzantine, oriental sphere. These were the arms of an Orthodox ruler whose kingdom was in Moldavia, many miles to the north. At first sight it seemed an unlikely place, this staunchly Saxon citadel, but on reflection the arms brought home the ever-shifting allegiances that plagued the whole area. Boian lay within the region of Cetatea de Baltă, which was for a time in the control of the Moldavian princes. Within the space of about 30 years, the ownership of Boian changed at least four times: Count Nicholas of Salzburg swapped it with the nobleman George of Ludbreg in the 1450s; another nobleman acquired it in the 1460s, and in 1488 Matthias Corvinus bestowed the territory on Stephen of Moldavia.

Within the precinct of the crumbling fortifications, it was hard to imagine that the grass was once neatly cut, and that careful stores of ham and grain were kept here until the late 1970s. The grain stored within the church walls in large wooden boxes, one for each family, with the number of their house painted on the side, was what kept these people in their remote village on the shifting

borders of an oriental prince's land from ruin. Rationed out week by week, it might just last the winter and keep the inhabitants of Boian from starvation, or guard it from the hungry stomachs of whichever army happened to be sweeping through the place that month.

The Saxons were not only under threat from the Tatars and Turks, but also regularly caught up in the fights and feuding of the Hungarian, Wallachian and Moldavian princes. The shifting alliances and fearful uncertainty of the times can be demonstrated clearly by looking at the fortunes of Dracula. After his brother and father were killed in 1446–7, possibly by Hunyadi, Dracula remained with his cousin Stephen of Moldavia during the years 1449–51. Yet when Stephen's own father Bogdan was assassinated in 1451, Stephen and Dracula left Moldavia for Transylvania to seek help from Hunyadi. During 1451–6, the Saxons of Sibiu gave refuge to Dracula, yet four years later he raided the town. The Saxons claim, in what is undoubtedly an exaggeration, that he arrived with 20,000 men and killed, impaled and maimed some 10,000 people. At about the same time, he also attacked Braşov and the surrounding villages, where, if the Saxon propaganda is to be believed, he embarked on an orgy of destruction, death and cruelty, impaling thousands of people. A year after Dracula's attack on Sibiu in 1460, he was accused of being in league with the Turks and plotting with them to attack Transylvania; it was at this point that Matthias Corvinus imprisoned him. Yet during this time he is thought to have married one of Matthias's cousins, converted to Catholicism and accompanied the king's brother on a campaign against the Turks. After his release, he returned to Sibiu – where 13 years previously he had supposedly slaughtered 10,000 inhabitants – and applied for permission to build a house. He lived there for two years before recapturing the throne of Wallachia.

In the Evangelical church in Sibiu is the tomb of Dracula's son and heir, Mihnea the Bad. He was assassinated by a Serb in the main square in 1509 after holding the throne for little more than a year – although this was quite long enough for him to be given the epithet 'the Bad'. The church holds a fascinating collection of monuments, including many fine Renaissance tombstones of worthy Saxon gentlemen with wonderful details of clothing, some retaining traces of their original paint. It is amusing to find among them – just a few tombstone slabs away from Dracula's son – a memorial to one of the great Saxon figures and patron of the arts during the seventeenth century, Count Valentin Franck von Frankenstein.

Herr Wagner opened the door to the church, his hands trembling as he did so. The interior was chill and damp. The lights were not working. Three ragged carpets, half rotted away with damp and neglect, hung over the side of the organ loft. The organ, although built only in 1942, was in the most pitiable state, with several of the pipes missing or leaning against each other. It was a frightening indication of how quickly neglect turns to rot.

As my eyes became accustomed to the low level of light, I noticed some fragments of wall painting next to a richly decorated late Gothic tabernacle some four metres high in the north wall of the chancel. Although they were in a bad state of repair, I could make out the figure of a woman with an elaborate crown on her head, representing Ecclesia, or the Church, with two smaller figures next to her; they were all that remained of the three theological virtues. The scene was set in the Renaissance interior of a castle, and one or two battlements were still visible. Above was a fragment from a separate scene, with branches of trees and a couple of heads. It was not until I climbed onto the choirstall opposite and stood at the same height as the picture that I could make out a forest of bodies being impaled on the thorny branches of trees.

Some men were pierced through their hands and feet, others through their stomachs and chests. Here was a church stamped with the desperation of life on the eastern-most edges of Europe in the late Middle Ages. The wall painting showing the horrid tormented forest was the visual manifestation of a real horror for the

Germans. The scene was similar in style to one in the great church at Mediaş, some 20 kilometres away, that has been dated to about 1520. At Mediaş, the paintings are much better preserved and are part of a large scheme that still exists over the central nave. There the viewer has to peer up at the legend, and although startling, its impact is diluted by the survival of so many other rich scenes from the life of Christ and the saints. Here in Boian, as practically the sole surviving fragment, the horrid scene in this sad and gloomy church brought home the full terror of life in a border country.

Right: *Wall painting at Boian showing men being impaled, a scene from the legend of the 10,000 martyrs. Impaling was the form of execution favoured by Vlad the Impaler 'Dracula'.*
Previous page, left: *Fragment of early 15th-century wall-painting from the Hungarian Unitarian church at Dârjiu (Székelyderzs) representing a scene from the legend of St Lászlo, revered as good and perfect a Christian king as Dracula was considered evil and heathen. The fortified church in the Hungarian Szekler area also contains a depiction of the 10,000 being impaled.*
Previous page, right: *Religious procession through Maramureş village on the feast of St John the Baptist, celebrated after epiphany on 7 January.*

This painting, as at Mediaş, is a depiction of the death of the 10,000 martyrs. This legend, dating from the twelfth century, tells how 10,000 Christian soldiers in Asia Minor, refusing to sacrifice to idols as required under Roman law, were condemned by the Emperor Hadrian to suffer all the torments of Christ and were crucified on Mount Ararat. As the martyrs were dying, they prayed to God that those who venerated their memory would receive God's protection, and a voice from heaven announced that their prayer would be granted. This legend became extremely popular in medieval Germany and is found in surviving fourteenth-century wall paintings on the Lower and Middle Rhine. Later Albrecht Dürer depicted the martyrs suffering many torments, some being put to the sword or thrown off cliffs onto spikes. In Carpaccio's version in the Uffizzi Gallery in Florence they are crucified.

Other existing wall paintings in Transylvania showing the martyrs being impaled can be found at Teaca (Tekendorf), dating from the last quarter of the fourteenth century, and in the Hungarian Unitarian church at Székelyderzs (Dârjiu) from 1419. On an altar panel from the church at Târnava (Großprobstdorf), near Mediaş, Christ on the Cross is shown surrounded by ten men, all of whom are impaled, a scene thought to date from the 1480s to 1490s.

In the way that medieval painters dressed the biblical characters in contemporary dress and put them in a landscape that they would recognise themselves, sitting on furniture they might have found in their houses or riding in carts they saw on the streets every day, so the painters depicted contemporary torments. This horrific form of death was all too familiar to the Saxons of Transylvania. Even if they had not had the misfortune to see anyone being impaled, they would certainly have heard or read about it, possibly in one of the blood-curdling pamphlets that were being circulated long after Dracula's death and well into the 1500s.

Dracula did not invent this particular form of punishment, and as can be seen from the dates of some of the surviving paintings of the 10,000 martyrs, the Saxons knew about it long before Dracula's birth. They equated it in their minds with a horrifying death inflicted on Christians by pagans. To the Saxons, Dracula, an Orthodox Christian, would have been considered to be no more a Christian than the heathens who martyred the 10,000 – hence the comment in one of the early German Dracula stories about him reforming his ways after he had become a Christian, meaning that he had converted to Catholicism, at the court of Matthias Corvinus.

It has been suggested that Dracula learned about impaling from the Turks when he and his brother were held hostage by the sultan as boys. The Tatars also used this form of torture. Dracula was not the only leader to use the punishment further west, however. Stephen the Great of Moldavia is said to have impaled captured Tatars, and in the kingdom of Hungary nine peasants who revolted against the nobility during the year 1437–8 were put on stakes.

The account of Dracula's attack on Braşov tells in chilling detail how he came 'early in the morning' and had men and women, young and old, impaled by St Jacob's chapel under the hill. He sat in the middle of the scene and 'ate his morning bread with much pleasure'. A pamphlet published in Nuremberg in 1491 has a woodcut showing Dracula feasting at a table with the bodies of those whom he had impaled all around him. There is gruesome speculation about how people were impaled, and how many men or horses it would take to do it. Dürer's painting may provide a clue as to how a large number of people could be impaled at one time – they would have been thrown off the side of a hill onto spikes. Perhaps this is why Dracula took his victims to the hill outside Braşov.

The light had almost gone and we did not wish to keep Herr Wagner from his evening chores any longer. A neighbour had agreed to put his cow in the shed when it came in from the fields, but Herr Wagner still had to milk it. In the past, as in all Saxon villages, a bell would have been rung at eight o'clock each night to warn the villagers that the cows should be home and all men and animals should be safely locked behind their gates. As elsewhere in the Saxon lands, there were few Saxons left to warn. The community at Boian possessed a bell with a Latin inscription expressing the wish that the king of glory would come with peace in the year of our lord 1477 – a year after Dracula was killed in a battle near Bucharest.

Boian felt like a brooding and tragic place now, but when I consulted Hermann Fabini's *Atlas of Transylvanian Saxon Fortified Churches and Villages*, a work of immense scholarship and dedication, there was no record that the village had ever been attacked by Tatars, Turks or Dracula. Two fires destroyed it, but both of these had come late in the village's history, in the eighteenth and nineteenth centuries. Peaceful settlements in the area, which seemed so lovely in their remote tranquillity, had suffered far more terrible histories. They were reminders of Pope Pius II's comment about Dracula: 'The Wallachian is still rotting in prison; a man of fine build and stature whose good looks seem worthy of a crown – how often does a man's appearance differ from his soul.'

The difference between the historical prince and the fictional count is not just one of rank, although Dracula really was a Transylvanian count – the Hungarian king had bestowed the title of Count of Amlaş and Făgăraş (Fogarasch) on his father, which Dracula duly inherited. The one impaled his victims, the other drank their blood. Bram Stoker never visited Transylvania and did his research in the British Library. He was much influenced by Emily Gerard, whose article on Transylvanian superstitions in the 1880s provided inspirational background material. She lived for several years in Sibiu as the wife of an officer in the Austro-Hungarian Army, and was fascinated by the customs of the inhabitants of Transylvania. She describes in some detail beliefs concerning, among others, werewolves and vampires. For her, Transylvania was the land of superstition. The fictional Jonathan Harker observes in his diary: 'I read that every known superstition in the world is gathered into the horseshoe of the Carpathians, as if it were the centre of some sort of imaginative whirlpool.'

Sabine Baring-Gould's *Book of Werewolves* (1865) also inspired Stoker. He discusses many stories from around the world about belief in werewolves and instances of lycanthropy, a medical condition where men (it usually is men) take on the characteristics of a wild animal. This is most commonly a wolf, hence the name of the condition from the Greek words *lukos*, wolf, and *anthropos*, man. The Reverend Baring-Gould gives just one account from Transylvania in a discussion about blood lust, where a person needs to taste the blood of another human being. He cites the notorious case of the late-sixteenth-century Transylvanian Countess Elisabeth Báthory, who was accused of torturing and killing hundreds of her maidservants. She was said to have drunk their blood as a beauty tonic to give her youthful looks. The stories about her are full of feverish sadomasochistic detail, and there is a sexual undercurrent to the whole account that is reminiscent of *Dracula*. Elisabeth Báthory received life imprisonment for her alleged crimes, and, suspiciously, all her estates were confiscated to the advantage of her sons-in-law, who initiated the case against her.

The first werewolves in literature are usually placed somewhere between the present Republic of Moldova (formerly Romanian Bessarabia) and the River Dniester in Russia. Herodotus tells how a tribe called the Neuri were rumoured to practise magic: 'for there is a story amongst the Scythians and the Greeks in Scythia that once a year every Neurian transforms into a wolf for a few days, and then turns back into a man again. I do not believe this tale, but all the same, they tell it and even swear to the truth of it.'

In Romania, the word *pricolici* is used for an evil or restless spirit of a person, usually after death, who

Left: *Sweeping the wooden church at the Greco-Catholic church in Ieud, in Maramureş. Rugs as well as embroidered cloths decorate this church.*
Right: *Detail of window with a cross behind it. Religious and magic belief suffuses everyday life in many villages.*

inhabits the body of an animal. Sometimes the man can take the form of a wolf or a dog. In one village the priest's daughter told me very seriously that although she did not believe in vampires or werewolves, she had heard women in her village say that some husbands turned into beasts when they were in bed, and every new wife should check her husband's feet at night before they went to sleep to make sure that they were not cloven. Emily Gerard tells the amusing anecdote of a botanist who was mistaken for a werewolf when he was seen crouching in a wolf-like position while collecting plants on a hillside. When he stood up, the peasants were even more alarmed, for it seemed to confirm their worst fears that here was a wolf who had just changed back into a man. The peasants rushed off after him, and as Emily Gerard observes, 'He might have fared badly indeed had he not succeeded in gaining a carriage on the highroad before his pursuers came up.'

Although there are many traditions and superstitions connected with the dead in Romania, it is the belief about vampires that has been the most notorious – largely, but not only, through the popularity of Stoker's novel. In all my travels in rural Transylvania, I never met a Romanian who admitted to believing in them, and the belief is said to be more prevalent in Serbia and in the region of Romania which borders it. Occasionally, however, there are stories in the Romanian press which show that the belief in vampires is far from dead. One concerned six men who were jailed for unlawful exhumation of a body. Believing that the man had returned from the dead to drink their blood at night, they were reported to have put stakes through its body and sprinkled garlic over it before putting it back in the grave. They then burnt his heart at a crossroads and drank the ashes from it, which they believed would protect them from the 'undead'. The dead man's daughter, who no longer lived in the village, had brought the complaint against them, but when other local people were questioned, they did not seem unduly scandalised by the accused men's action. Some admitted that they knew of other cases where this had happened, one man even confessing that he had drunk the ashes of a dead man to protect himself from being haunted by him.

Drinking ashes or cinders in water is a common magical antidote in Transylvania, although it is more usual to use a match, or ashes from the fire, rather than human remains. When my cousin became ill while staying with me in the Apuseni, my first reaction was that she had eaten something that had disagreed with her; our hostess's view was that someone had put the evil eye on her. She gave her a glass of water over which she whispered a secret incantation, and obliged my cousin to light and blow out a match nine times over it before stirring in the ashes and drinking it. Nine has a special significance and power in popular belief as it is three times three, and three is the symbol of the Trinity. It was fascinating to see this piece of folk medicine being applied, although my cousin did not feel much better as a result of it. Despite the best efforts of the Communists to suppress religious and superstitious beliefs, somehow they survived in a population where, until 1949, 80 per cent of the population lived in rural communities. Even now, agricultural land accounts for 62 per cent of Romania's surface area, and nearly half of the population is engaged in some form of agricultural work. Many town dwellers are only first generation and have preserved the superstitions and beliefs of their parents and grandparents.

Vampires were believed to be people who had died in unfortunate circumstances and returned from the grave in human or animal form to cause mayhem. As the recent vampire scandal showed, the only way to get rid of them was to exhume their undecayed, still bloody bodies from

Right: *Geese waddle past a wayside cross. Crosses are often found at boundaries and crossroads, as in magic belief such areas are potentially dangerous. Men involved in a recent vampire case allegedly burnt a man's heart at a crossroads.*

the grave and either drive a stake through them, behead them, or cut out their hearts and burn them.

There are a few obscure early references to vampires, but it was only from the sixteenth century that there are any clear accounts. A Hungarian scholar, Gábor Klaniczay, has suggested that vampire beliefs were peculiarly attractive to the eighteenth-century mind and came to take the place of witches in people's fantasies. Bloodsucking was a quasi-medical concept which provided a more rational explanation than witches' spells for acts of supposed magic. For those in the enlightened West, the stories provided a frisson of exoticism and a deeply erotic subtext. Vampires were like incubi or succubi, demons who took the shape of men or women respectively to have sexual intercourse with people while they slept. Whereas witch-hunters of the past had conjured up feverish images of witches having intercourse with the Devil, the women in question were usually poor, haggard old women; now this picture was replaced by the idea of vampires preying on innocent, usually young women. In vampire belief, Death embraced these women and drank their blood in

Left: *Lighting candles in the churchyard on All Souls' Day, the 'Day of the Dead'. Many superstitions are connected with the dead, vampire belief being one of them.*

order to be rejuvenated by them. It was a new and vivid portrayal of the strong attraction between Eros and Thanatos, love and death, and a theme exploited so vividly in *Dracula*.

In rural Romania, however, vampire belief has less to do with sexual fantasy than with belief in the undead and concern about those weary souls who are somehow trapped between one world and the next. According to Orthodox belief, the soul does not leave the body until 40 days after death. So there are services (called *parastas*) 40 days after the burial to celebrate the soul's departure to heaven. *Parastas* are also held after six months, nine months and on each anniversary of the person's death. The *parastas* should be held on Saturday, on the day when Christ rested in the tomb, although nowadays such rituals usually take place after the service on Sunday, either in church or around the grave. The family brings a special round loaf into which a candle is inserted and prayers are said around it. This loaf is then distributed after the service and considered especially beneficial because it has been blessed. Sometimes *coliva*, the basic ingredients of which are boiled wheatgerm (to signify resurrection) mixed with nuts and honey, is also distributed.

At the beginning of November, on the eve of All Souls' Day (the date is not fixed in the Orthodox calendar as it must fall on a Saturday), women and children clean their family graves, repaint the crosses, light incense and candles, and decorate the graves with flowers, sometimes spending the night in the churchyard. On All Souls' day, known in Maramureş as *Luminaţie*, or 'Illumination', a service is held in the cemetery to commemorate the dead. Ritual loaves are placed on a table in front of the priest, together with a piece of paper listing all the dead members in the family of each villager. The priest reads out the names provided in one long, sonorous chant. The whole cemetery is lit by the candles on the graves, and after the service food and drink is solemnly shared. In villages in Maramureş, 'tables of ancestors' are still used for placing the food for a feast after the commemoration of a service for the dead. Always, outside every Orthodox church are two trays of candles, one on the left side of the door and the other on the right: one for the living and one for the dead. Two sets of souls existing side by side – one on this earth, the other in heaven. In some villages, the names of all the living and all the dead are read out in church by the priest every Sunday, adding greatly to the length of the service.

A friend from Bucharest said that when her grandmother died in Bucharest, her family covered the mirrors in the house. They did this from the belief that if her dead grandmother's soul caught sight of herself in the mirror, she could have become trapped on earth and thus a ghost. Ghosts, it is believed, cause such a fright that a person's face can become twisted at the sight of them, as western children are sometimes warned will happen to them if they are caught pulling faces when the wind changes.

When my friend Mircea's mother died in the Transylvanian village where I lived for a time, the female relations washed and dressed the corpse and laid it in an open coffin in the main room of the house so that her family and neighbours might visit her for the last time. Ileana, Mircea's wife, said that if someone died with their eyes open, you put coins on the eyelids to shut them, and if a person died with their mouth open, you tied a scarf round their jaw and head to shut it; she mimicked the action of the jaw snapping shut, and laughed. The mourners sat round the edges of the room and talked to each other, reminiscing about the dead person and recalling memorable events from their life. In some regions of Romania, such as Maramureş, the women still sing laments, but this had never been the custom in Mircea's village, at least within living memory.

Like a wedding, a funeral is an event in which the wider community plays a part. On more than one occasion while travelling through Maramureş looking for some church or other, I have heard women keening.

It is something strange and unexpected, a haunting sound that belongs to an alien world. And as often happens when a wedding is taking place, visitors may be invited to a funeral, even tourists passing briefly through the village. Westerners, being generally squeamish about death, which is usually a discreet matter, may instinctively decline the invitation, feeling that they should not intrude on a stranger's private grief. Yet to turn down an invitation to a funeral feast would be seen as an affront to the dead person's soul. Marriage and death are both viewed as important facts of life, solemn rituals that are public events. At the feast after the funeral, called a *pomană*, the dead person's favourite food is served. Each guest receives a small loaf of bread, a candle and some wine.

On the day of the funeral, the priest comes to the house and everyone gathers in the courtyard around the coffin and says prayers. Then the coffin is carried to church to be buried. 'After the funeral, you put a full glass of water out on the window ledge and food on the plate off which the priest has eaten in the drawer underneath the table. After six weeks you throw them away. But only a little water remains after that time,' Ileana said. These precautions are taken in case the dead person needs sustenance during the 40 days he or she remained on earth after death. It is said that during this time the soul must travel to all the places it has been when alive. For the people in the villages, that would be a sufficient amount of time to visit the house where they were born if they no longer lived there, to go into the surrounding forest, perhaps, and the local town. The men would have plenty of time left to go to the barracks where they did national service, and the women would be able to revisit the monastery where they once went on pilgrimage. But how would more well-travelled souls manage? Might they be condemned to wander the earth as ghosts?

In churchyards occasionally a fir tree hung with ribbons, similar to one traditionally carried in wedding processions, stands at the head of a grave. In the words of the 'Song of the Fir Tree', a folk song collected by Tiberiu Alexandru:

Oh, fir tree
Who was it told you
To come down to us
From a rocky place
To a marshy place
From the rocks
To the water here?
The one who told me
Was one who has left
And who needs me
For shade in summer
For shelter in winter.

It was considered a particular tragedy if a villager of childbearing age died unmarried, for it meant that they had not been able to take their full place in the community before death. When this happened, a special ceremony – a 'wedding of the dead' – was performed, as it was feared that the dead person would not be able to rest, remaining unfulfilled socially and sexually: another manifestation of the uneasy attraction between love and death.

A whole ritual once surrounded the cutting down and adornment of the wedding/funeral tree, in which the village girls would come to meet the boys who had cut down the tree and sing the 'Song of the Fir Tree', in which the tree expressed sorrow that it had been cut down, not as a sign of joy for a wedding as it hoped, but for a funeral as a mark of grief:

If I had understood
I would never have sprung up
If I had known
I would not have grown.

All that remained of the ritual in many Transylvanian

villages was this ribbon tree, although very elaborate 'weddings of the dead' still took place in Maramureş. Through the ribbon tree, they were married to nature for all eternity. As a funeral lament from Vrancea states:

O man, O tree,
Do not pity yourself,
Do not bemoan your fate;
But rather rejoice,
For though your root
May have died in the earth
You have struck new roots in heaven.

Just as one could be married to a tree in death, so in certain circumstances could a woman be married to one in life. In the past, if an unmarried girl became pregnant and her lover would not marry her, it was the custom for her to be taken to a tree and bound to it. Thus married to the tree, she was entitled to cover her head with a scarf and be accorded the same status as other married women in the village.

Nearly 50 years of Communism had succeeded only in driving people's fears and beliefs underground. Romanian Communism did not manage to provide much, but it had at least offered stability of sorts. Since the revolution, people's lives have been much less certain. There has been an explosion of interest in religion, as well as in spells, fortune-tellers and witches – perhaps as a result of the need to fill a void after the collapse of Communism and as a means of reassurance at a time of uncertainty. New churches and monasteries are springing up as fast as new houses.

A type of booklet called 'The Talisman' is commonly found on sale at monasteries and from stalls at country fairs and festivals. As the name suggests, it contains a special protective prayer which it claims can help women during labour, protect a baby against illnesses and accidents, and bring it luck. The prayer can also be used as a charm against a number of illnesses, including epilepsy, and as a protection for houses against flooding or being destroyed by enemies. The talisman I bought

Right: *Carving wooden crosses in Maramureş.*
Following page, left: *The bride's mother offering cakes to the priest at a wedding in Maramureş. Marriage is of enormous social significance. If a young man or woman dies unmarried, it is feared that they will become restless spirits and a 'wedding of the dead' is performed.*
Following page, right: *While the bride is being dressed, the women sing. In rhyming couplets they tell her how hard life will be as a married woman. The bride is expected to cry, and, unsurprisingly, she does.*

dated from the sixteenth century, but here it was, still being printed, with no suggestion that the reader need not be protected 'against fires, drowning and witches'. Such was the eternal nature of the Romanian peasant and the Orthodox Church. In the front of the edition was a list of other works by the 'Food for the Soul' publishing house, including one called 'How to escape from spells and magic and pagan objects'.

Even in matters of religion and magic, there is a constant struggle between the old and the new, the East and the West. Witches advertise their services in magazines and on television. Every so often there are reports that officials are pursuing witches to pay their taxes. And the witches duly respond that they have issued curses for life over the local mayor, or taxman, or whoever is trying to pursue them to fill in their tax returns for their work in casting spells or telling fortunes. Far from frowning on this sort of belief, the Romanian Orthodox Church encourages it by issuing booklets of counter-spells for those who consider themselves bewitched. In the villages, people who have experienced personal misfortune, often of a sort that puts them in a position of social embarrassment in the village – a man who has been jilted by his bride or parents whose son has a drink problem – will often attribute the cause to supernatural reasons. They will claim to have been cursed, and if homemade spells do not remedy the situation, they consult the priest. He takes the place of a psychiatrist in the community, although he encourages his parishioners to fast and pray rather than lie on a couch.

I never knowingly met a vampire or indeed anyone who admitted to being a witch, although plenty of people claimed to have been cursed by witches and several taught me certain charms to undo curses. But I did meet a Hungarian hermit who more than exceeded my expectations. His beard was long and unkempt and his dark hair stuck out on end, as though bristling with static electricity. It was the type of hair that might quickly become matted with locusts and wild honey in the wilderness. Born in a small village, he had become a hermit about 20 years previously, when, during a violent storm, the metal rosary beads he was wearing had miraculously acted as a lightning conductor and saved his life.

My friend Csaba said that the hermit had once played the trumpet in a band, and that when he first became a hermit it had been very beautiful to hear the sound of his trumpet echoing through the mountains. I asked Csaba what kind of band the hermit had played in.

'It was like your fire brigade bands,' he replied.

I had never heard of fire brigades forming bands in Britain, and wondered how they had acquired this reputation in Transylvania.

During Ceauşescu's time, the hermit had lived a genuinely isolated life, sleeping in a coffin and seeing almost no one except the local priest. When the outspoken Catholic priest had word that the Romanian secret police, the *Securitate*, wanted to get hold of him for a beating or interrogation, as they did quite regularly in the years leading up to the revolution, he would escape up the mountain to hide with the hermit and no one would be able to find him. Csaba commented, though, that people in the town had been muttering recently about the hermit's luxurious lifestyle, and there were even rumours that he had acquired a mobile phone. Some believed the rot had set in when he had been taken to Germany after the revolution to be shown off as Europe's last living hermit.

Right: *Ruins of the former Cistercian abbey at Cârţa (Kerz). Founded by monks from Pontigny in France in about 1202, it was destroyed by Turks in the fifteenth century. The church choir became a Saxon Lutheran church.*

Left: *Wool hanging out to dry on fences.*

Chapter 3

The Wild Places

Everyone who lived in the Apuseni Mountains was afraid of bears – much more so than wolves – and they were considered to be evil. There are thought to be about 5,000 bears in Romania, an estimated 50 per cent of Europe's bear population. Most of them live in the Carpathian and Apuseni Mountains, and the villagers share their environment – and their food – with the bears.

There is something strangely human about bears, which are able to stand on two legs and walk on the soles of their feet. Living for up to 30 years, a male bear can weigh as much as 350 kilos, females up to 200 kilos. It is unsurprising that there are many legends and fairytales about them, such as the Grimm brothers' 'Bearskin' and 'Snow White and Rose Red'. At the end of both stories, the bears magically shed their skin, revealing themselves as men cursed and condemned to live out their lives as these solitary animals, shunned by humans.

Bears were certainly considered unlucky in that they were a threat to livestock, especially in late summer and autumn when they had to eat large quantities of food in order to build up the layer of fat that was essential for surviving their hibernation in winter. On one of many visits to the Apuseni, I climbed up to see my friend Ileana's mother, who lived in a house high up the valley on the side of a mountain. The old woman was standing outside her house, looking tired and anxious, and could only address us in a whisper. She had lost her voice the previous night because she had been shouting at a bear. Unfortunately, it had managed to kill one of her pigs and severely injure the other. She was so terrified, she said, she had screamed and screamed at the bear until eventually it had run off. She was shaken by the incident, by the violent intrusion on her land. The loss of the pigs meant that there would be none to fatten in time for Christmas. Ileana's mother had done the right thing. Making a lot of noise was by far the safest way to get rid of a bear. If she had thrown missiles, she would have risked hurting it, and having an injured bear on her property would have been just about as dangerous as if she had disturbed a female bear with a cub.

During the 1980s, when the bear population reached its height – an estimated 8,000 animals – four people on average were killed by bears each year. Ceauşescu was a keen hunter who liked to compete with fellow Communist leaders such as Zhivkov of Bulgaria and Tito of Yugoslavia for the biggest trophies. Despite all his efforts and enthusiasm, he was reputed to be a terrible shot, although it is no easier to establish the truth about Ceauşescu now that he is dead than when he was alive. What is certain is that thanks to his ban on hunting – except for himself and favoured friends – the bear population soared. He set up feeding places for bears in the mountains and had cubs raised artificially to stock underpopulated areas. After the revolution, because of this overpopulation, bears were poached and poisoned as well as hunted under licence and the numbers decreased. Under revised hunting laws in line with European Union legislation, wolves and bears are now protected species. Licences may be issued to hunt them if there is proof of a high damage to livestock in an area, and managers of accredited hunting territories are allowed to issue a certain quota of individual permits for hunting wolves, bears and lynx. Such licences can be lucrative, as foreign sportsmen and, increasingly, rich Romanians are prepared to pay handsomely – as much as 8,000 to 10,000 Euros – to shoot bears.

For the past few years, some bears – which can consume up to 40 kilos of food at one meal – have come down from the forest to forage in dustbins in towns such as Braşov. The bears have become a tourist attraction, with people bringing food for them as though they were ducks on an ornamental pond. Wolves, too, have been seen in the town. The Carpathian Large Carnivore Project, which ran from 1993 to 2003 monitoring wolves, bears and lynx in the Carpathians, put a radio-collar on a wolf and managed to film it foraging at night in rubbish dumps on the outskirts of Braşov, like urban foxes. In the mountains it was shy of people and evasive, yet in the city it adapted its behaviour, looking right and left before crossing the road and showing itself indifferent to people as it ran along the pavements like a domestic dog.

In the Apuseni Mountains, however, people retained their instinctive fear about wolves and bears, and sometimes the attitudes of the town and country clashed. A bear had been killing horses in the mountain pastures, but animal rights' organisations had objected to a proposed bear hunt, claiming it was necessary to prove that the bear the hunters shot was the one that had caused the damage. The villagers were also upset. How did they expect such proof to be obtained? Without their horses, the peasants would be unable to bring wood from the forest or take their goods to sell at market. No one would give them any compensation for their loss.

We once went to visit the family of Ileana's son-in-law, who lived in a remote farmstead in a neighbouring valley. There was no means of announcing our visit, as only three people in the village had telephones at the time – the policeman, the doctor and the priest. Until recently, mobile phones were also unheard-of luxuries in this area, and only well-off people such as the baker or

Right: *The thousands of bears and wolves in Romania pose a threat to livestock, and flocks are guarded closely.*

forester could afford them. When we arrived, a fire was smouldering in one of the fields. They were burning the remains of a bear which had been attacking livestock and which they had shot the previous night. It was surprising to see that its whole carcass was being burned. One would expect that the men who shot it might have wanted to keep the skin – if not as a trophy, then to use the fur for hats, clothes or rugs. In a society where nothing went to waste, the meat should also be enjoyed. But no, the bear was being burned because it was *rău*, or bad.

At first, it appeared that they were doing this because they believed the bear to be evil, or they considered it bad to kill a bear. Stories about bears in northern Europe are full of reference to their human qualities, and they are traditionally respected as the equals of man in the forest and so accorded particular respect. Certain peoples of Central Asia and Siberia held ritual services in honour of bears that they killed, and the North American Sioux made cloaks out of dead bear hides and danced for days to appease a bear's spirit. Later, on reflection, it was clear that one reason the Romanian bear was being burned was to remove any evidence. If the man who shot it had not obtained a licence, then he might be in trouble with the police and liable to pay a large fine. And this would indeed be 'bad'.

Elsewhere in Europe, the brown bear is facing extinction. In the central Pyrenees there are an estimated five bears, while in Italy just four are left in the southern Alps and a maximum of 80 survive in the Apennines. There are fewer than 100 in the whole of Spain, and in Norway they became extinct during the 1980s, although farmers are regularly harassed by them coming over the border from Russia. To the dismay of French farmers, two Slovenian bears were recently introduced into the Pyrenees in an attempt to re-establish the bear population there. The reintroduction of a further three was halted, however, when attempts were made to kill the first two imported bears.

There were plans to reintroduce wolves into parts of Europe where they were dying out or extinct. Perhaps children are scared by different bogeymen nowadays, and other monsters have made their lairs in the human psyche. But there were sufficient numbers of terrifying wolves in the stories with which I grew up for it to seem perverse to encourage creatures of such savage cunning back into the countryside. Were we such confident masters of our environment, had we tamed it so completely, that we were confident we could control wild animals? Or perhaps it was because people did, deep down, still identify with wolves that they wanted to see them back.

The ancient geographer Strabo wrote that the Dacians, the original inhabitants of Romania, once called themselves 'Daoi', which has been linked with the Phrygian word for wolf, *daos*, and the Illyrian word *dhaunos*, of the same meaning. On Trajan's Column in Rome, built in 114 AD, which records the Dacians' defeat at the hands of the Romans, there is a depiction of the Dacians' strange battle standard. It has a wolf-like head attached to a long bag. When the wind blew through the animal's mouth, its body became inflated and let out an eerie sound like the howl of a wolf.

In contrast to bears, wolves were perceived as less of a threat to the villagers. When asked about them, people's first reaction was to say that there were no longer any wolves, and they had to think hard to remember incidents when wolves had killed sheep. Mircea then said that when he was eight years old, his aunt was looking out of the window one day when she saw a strange dog appear in the yard. But when she went outside to shoo it away, she saw that it was a wolf, so she threw her coat over it and ran screaming back into the house. He added that when he was young – in the late 1950s – his mother did not like him and his brothers and

Left: *Steep roof of a barn in the Apuseni Mountains used for storing hay and animals.*

sisters to go alone into the forest in winter and spring for fear of bears and wolves.

Some people had distant memories, passed on from their parents, of packs of wolves running through villages in bad winters devouring everything in sight. It is true that there were many more wolves about in the past. During the 1950s, the wolf population grew to more than 4,000 and became a threat to livestock. The government instituted a cull, and by the late 1960s the number had declined to an estimated 1,500. Since then, the population has begun to recover, and figures from 1996 put the number at 3,100.

A friend of the village doctor from Bucharest, who was an enthusiastic potholer, went to collect a group who had been exploring a nearby cave in the early hours of the morning. The boys were late coming back and he was bored. So, when he saw some lights between the trees, he got out of his car and began to walk towards them, thinking they were the cavers' lamps. As he got nearer, he was puzzled to see that there were more lights than there

Left: *Shepherd near Sibiu with one of his dogs which are primarily used for protection against wild animals.*
Right: *Although much about their lives is traditional, shepherds are now more likely to keep in touch by walkie-talkie or mobile phone than alpine horn.*

were boys out caving. He shone his torch towards them, and suddenly realised that he was looking not at lamps but at pairs of eyes. 'I ran back to the car and locked myself in,' he continued. 'I lit a cigarette and put some music on loud. I was very agitated.'

The people who had most reason to be nervous about wolves were shepherds. During the first summer that I spent in the Apuseni, I would ask people where the shepherds were and they would smile and say, '*Sus, sus*' (above, above), as though they were angels. And this is a little how I thought of them, as people whose lives lay closer to heaven than earth, and who, until they came down from the high passes at the beginning of autumn, were invisible but whose benign presence was enjoyed in the shape of cheese and milk. The doctor told me how beautiful it was when out in the mountains in summer to listen to the sound of the *tulnic*, a slender type of alpine horn, as it echoed through the hills, and to hear some faraway shepherds respond to it on a distant mountain.

A vast mythology surrounded shepherds. All sorts of strange stories were told about them – tales of jealous sheep and immaculately impregnated sheep. Although it was usually women who were accused of witchcraft, in the rarer cases where men were involved, it always seemed to be ones who lived high in the mountains or who were shepherds.

Shepherds were also the butt of lewd jokes, predictably about their isolation and proximity to sheep. In other parts of the country, I came across stories of the *Fata Pădurii*, the Forest Maiden, who is variously described as a beautiful woman without a back or one who can change shape at whim. She tempts shepherds to make love to her and, as a reward, leads them to better pastures. To protect their men against her pernicious influence, women were warned to rub their men's bodies with garlic, candle wax, and the juice of the greater celandine. Such a remedy sounded more like a punishment for being led astray by a backless woman than a deterrent. As every countrywoman would know, the greater celandine has a yellow juice that is acrid and poisonous, and can be used as a caustic for burning away warts. In a variant of 'Hansel and Gretel' from the Maramureş region, it is the Forest Maiden who lures the children to her cottage, which is covered with the peasant's festive treats of pancakes and sausages.

I was not sure what these mystical shepherds would look like, but when I first met one, walking in the Bucegi Mountains high in the Carpathians, he was a young man with a face as red and shiny as an apple polished for harvest festival, whose 30-odd sheep were surrounded by no fewer than 10 bear-like dogs. As any Romanian walker will warn, Romanian sheepdogs are trained to

kill. Everyone warned hikers to watch out for them while walking in the mountains because they were man-eaters, trained to kill any living creature that might threaten their flock. Large dogs with light-coloured coats, they are more the size of Old English sheepdogs but leaner and without such cute looks. They are similar to Pyrenean mountain dogs and must be closely related. The doctor said that the only way to deal with them was to carry a stick in one hand and drag a branch behind you with the other. This was because the sheepdogs' ace tactic was to attack suddenly at the rear, so the theory was that if they saw something trailing behind, they would be confused and stall their attack.

When watching these dogs one afternoon, I could not help feeling cheated. Outside the shepherds' summer camp a couple of hours before sunset, there were hundreds of sheep, a few cows and at least a dozen dogs. One shepherd had begun to milk the cows for the evening, and the others were running about rounding up the sheep. Did the dogs help? Did they move as much as a centimetre, while the shepherds whistled and raced about energetically? On the contrary, the sheepdogs sat in their various corners of the pasture, like generals watching manoeuvres from elevated ground. Only when the shepherds managed to put almost all the sheep in their pen did two or three dogs deign to get up and run a round a bit, as though putting on a show in the vain hope that no one noticed their shirking. The fact is that these are primarily guard dogs, and they had taken up position on each corner of the pen to watch out for any sign of attack. Presumably, as sheepdogs in the West have not had to worry about wolf attacks for about 300 years, they have been trained to help their masters in other shepherding activities. There will be much retraining to do if schemes to reintroduce wolves in the wild are successful.

Mioriţa, the most celebrated of all Romanian poems, tells the story of a shepherd who is warned by one of his sheep, called Mioriţa, that his fellow shepherds have plotted to kill him. Instead of taking action, the shepherd accepts his fate, telling the sheep to make sure that his murderers bury him near the sheepfold with his favourite flutes, so that his flock will be able to mourn his death. He asks Mioriţa to tell his mother that he has gone to marry a princess at the gates of heaven rather than reveal the fact that his marriage has taken place with the earth.

Do not tell her, dear lamb, that at my wedding
A star fell
Or that my guests were fir and maple trees.
And my priests were high mountains
A thousand birds my musicians
And the stars lit my way.

The philosopher Emil Cioran (son of an Orthodox priest who, like so many Romanian intellectuals in the early decades of the twentieth century, settled in France) regarded this poem, however, as 'an open wound in the Romanian soul', the fatal resignation which it exemplifies a national curse. 'To consider folk values as ends in themselves', he wrote, 'is to fail in the ascent towards culture, for a people that has created only a popular culture has not yet crossed the threshold to history.'

The shepherds from the area around Sibiu were mythically prosperous. Some were said to have their own helicopters. In Ceauşescu's time, their remote lives and knowledge of the high mountain passes which crossed forgotten borders gave them an independence denied to the rest of the population. In the late 1980s, two shepherds arrived over the border in Hungary to claim asylum together with a flock of 300 sheep.

The Apuseni Mountains also occasionally provided refuge from a few of the indignities and insanities of Communism. During the 1980s, Romania suffered from food shortages caused because Ceauşescu, determined to pay off the national debt, exported almost everything that was produced, leaving the country short of even the most basic products. Food, electricity and heating were rationed, and people in rural areas were obliged to give produce to the state in order to obtain vital coupons to buy bread, oil, rice and sugar. For example, they were supposed to surrender a surplus calf or piglet to the state. 'So,' the doctor said with a smile, 'there were lots of bones lying about the caves round here, as you can imagine. People had to dispose of their animals in secret and, if challenged, claim that they had fallen sick and died. The only good thing about it', he continued, 'was that there was a lot of black market meat about which was much cheaper than now.'

Surrounded by mountains and forests, Mircea and Ileana came from a village that lay in deepest outlaw country. Formed out of limestone, the whole region was riddled with caves, tunnels and gorges, strange dips and hollows. There was a place called the *lumea pierdută*,

Right: *Woman outside a wooden house in the foothills of the Apuseni Mountains.*
Previous page, left: *Many village streets remain unmetalled and easier to navigate on foot than by car.*
Previous page, right: *With small plots of land and no money to buy machinery, many people reverted to ancient farming methods after the revolution in 1989.*

which means the 'lost world', a mysterious area full of pits and sinkholes and underground rivers. One might imagine that it received this name because of all the caves and limestone formations, but really it was because the Austro-Hungarians had deforested the region so severely in the nineteenth century that all vegetation and wildlife died.

Within the many caves in the area, it was not uncommon to find the remains of prehistoric animals such as giant cave bears. Some caves were associated with famous fugitives who were said to have sheltered there. The Romanian word for an outlaw is *haiduc*, and there are many songs and poems about these men, who in folk memory have attained a similar status to Robin Hood. One of Romania's most celebrated revolutionaries, Avram Iancu, who led the Romanians against the Hungarians during the 1848 uprisings, was born in the Apuseni, and he used his knowledge of the surrounding landscape to confound his enemies.

Left: *Selling a pig at market in Maramureş.*
Following page, left: *Protective crosses are painted on the insides and outsides of houses, on barns, cowsheds and bread ovens.*
Following page, right: *Sheepfold equipped with all the buckets and sieves necessary to make cheeses.*

Many people from the valleys took to the caves and forests when they could not or would not pay the taxes imposed on them by their Austrian or Hungarian overlords in the eighteenth century. They lived harsh lives on the edge of the forest, gradually moving higher up the mountains as the population expanded and the need to harvest more wood grew. They lived in a cluster of small wooden houses in forest clearings, known as a *crâng*. People owed all their loyalty to those in their *crâng* rather than to people in other settlements or villages, and this is still true today, although individuals are increasingly dependent on the outside world. Every summer, the foresters go even higher into the mountains and live with their families and domestic animals in temporary settlements called *mutătoare*, which means 'changing from one place to the other'. The structures are made entirely of wood and provide the most basic type of shelter, yet each family takes care to nail protective crosses onto the outside of the buildings, especially the bread ovens. When the nearest permanent settlement is several hours' walk away, everyone makes sure that they are as self-sufficient as possible, and their food is obtained from their own animals, their fields or the forest.

Although no longer classified as outlaws, people who live in this region are still proud of being *Moţi*, the name given to the inhabitants of the Apuseni Mountains. The men once wore their hair long and braided in a single plait, which they laid over their shoulder in front. But only unmarried girls, and the occasional priest, wear their hair long now. Certainly, the Moţi remain closed and on the whole suspicious of outsiders. They did not gossip about their own people and were wary of telling strangers information about their beliefs. I spent long periods of time over several years among them, and although I became good friends with one particular family who were infinitely kind and generous, it was difficult to gather from anyone certain types of information, such as those about magic beliefs and rituals, even though this knowledge certainly still existed. Only those who had left the village long ago, and who no longer felt a part of the community, were willing to talk and gossip in a relaxed way.

The Moţi as a whole were as suspicious of change within their own community as they were of outsiders, and despite the poverty in which most of them lived, they were less likely to travel abroad in search of work than Romanians from other regions. Those who sought work outside the region tended to do so only for limited periods, and would then return.

In an area where cash was in such short supply, the Moţi still operated a barter system, trading wood for grain. Every spring and summer, Ileana's younger

brother Marinel loaded his wagon with timber and barrels, which he made in sets of five, fitting perfectly into each other like Russian dolls. He sold them at farms or markets, travelling up to 100 kilometres away. He occasionally received cash but was often paid in kind with grain or tools. When out on the road, men slept in their wagons. Mindful always of the evil eye, they felt uneasy among strangers and wary of falling among thieves.

Marinel had built the cart himself in the style of all the wagons in the area. The carriage was little more than a long wooden trough that could be fitted onto wheels in the summer and transferred to a sledge in winter. When it rained, he fixed a canvas hood over the top, so it looked like he was about to set off on the Oregon Trail. Marinel would sing as he travelled, in the same gently coaxing voice that he had when he spoke. One song had a wistful melody; it was a plaintive song of the type called *doină* in Romanian, inspired by the melancholy spirit of longing that Romanians call *dor*, a yearning for something or someone that one may perhaps never have or find. This spirit infuses much Romanian culture and is akin to the element of fatal passivity which Emil Cioran so despaired of in *Mioriţa*. Marinel said that his song was very old, and all the men in the area with carts like his sang it on their journeys:

'Little bay horse with the unusual mane,
Take me in your saddle through the countryside.'
'I will take you because you are not heavy,
It is your character that weighs heavy.
You go to all the inns,
At all of them I stop for you
So that you can drink with proud girls.
I fight with the rain
So that you can stay inside with proud girls,
And the horse has nothing on its back.'

As he held a top note, he would give his head a little shake from side to side and smile. His horses, Radu and Dinu, would swish their tails, twitching the tassels of red wool that were plaited into them to ward off the evil eye. He also tied tassels onto their bridles for good measure. Every year, Marinel's horses went through at least 100 horseshoes, made by the gypsies who lived on the outskirts of the village. He shoed them himself, using different nails according to the season: long and light ones for summer, and for winter heavy-duty nails with bigger heads. He hung his horses' bridles, red tassels still fixed to them, outside the stable alongside two wooden saddles, a pommel at each end, which looked as though they could have been suspended there for 400 years or more. Adjoining the stable was a room filled with the sweet, reassuring smell of hay and fir tree branches on which Marinel fed the horses. The wooden ladder to the hayloft looked like a living thing, as though the uncarved branches might burst into leaf in spring. One could imagine Odysseus using such a ladder to climb up to the bed that he made for Penelope. Radu and Dinu snorted as they champed on the mixture of fir tree branches and hay which certainly smelled delectable.

The local diet was very plain with a limited choice of vegetables, as it was hard to grow much in the mountains. Fresh fruit was available only in the summer when raspberries, strawberries and bilberries grew wild, and women and girls would rise before dawn to walk miles high into the forests to search for them. Only a handful would be eaten fresh. The rest was made into jam and syrups, or mixed with alcohol to keep the families' spirits up during the long winter months. It was customary to fast in preparation for the many feast days in the Orthodox calendar and also every Wednesday and Friday. On fasting days, no meat or dairy products were eaten. Fasting certainly performed a useful psychological function, providing the promise of a spiritual reward for those who might otherwise have had to deny themselves out of necessity. Soup, eggs, fresh tangy cow or sheep cheese, raw garlic and bread were the staples, supplemented with the odd piece of

pork or chicken, carrots or potatoes from the garden, and herbs from the meadows.

Bread had a special significance. It was essential for the living and an essential part of the ritual to honour the dead. Wheatgerm was a sign of hope and resurrection. Its importance was appreciated particularly in an area where wheat was not grown and had to be bought from outside. Down in the village, a large and successful bakery supplied the needs of those who lived in the valley, but in the mountains everyone baked their own bread in primal ovens, like something seen in a reconstruction of an ancient Celtic settlement. No one here ate brown or wholemeal bread. Ileana wrinkled up her nose in disgust when I mentioned it, and the village bakery produced only large round white loaves. It brought to mind Heidi trying to smuggle back stale white rolls from Frankfurt, which she had faithfully stored up for weeks, to her grandmother in the Alps. The bread oven was kept outside the house in its own small wooden shelter with a cross nailed on the roof to bless it.

In an environment where everything was put to use and everyone lived so close to the earth, people still used a

Left: *Bread – essential food for the living and an important part of the ritual to honour the dead. The inhabitants of the Apuseni still barter wood for wheat.*

Left: *Using an old threshing machine, made when Transylvania was still part of the Austro-Hungarian Empire.*
Right: *Back-breaking work, especially on steep pastures.*

number of natural remedies. Some were more efficacious than others. Many flowers were collected and dried for use as teas, one of the most popular being St John's Wort *(Hypericum perforatum)*, used by the ancient Greeks for the treatment of wounds and gout and in the West as an anti-depressant, where it is nicknamed 'Nature's Prozac'. Caraway was mixed with pure alcohol and sugar to make the local winter drink for men, fittingly called *crampă*, and cabbage was always served with caraway, presumably because of its carminative effect.

Baron von Campenhausen, 'a major of cavalry in the service of his Imperial Majesty and member of several academic and learned societies', notes in his book about the region, published in 1808, that the Bessarabian Moldavians had a remedy for intermittent fevers which he claimed to have witnessed the success of on several occasions. They boiled a certain quantity of sheep's dung in milk and, after straining the mixture through a sieve, gave it to the patient to drink. The Moţi did not know this particular remedy but volunteered another recipe. A hot poultice of horse manure was good for a cold on the chest. And if someone had a very bad fever – 'but it had to be a really bad one,' a friend's mother emphasised, her dark eyes shining with good humour – 'you should mash up the dung, then wrap it in a cloth and twist and twist very tight, straining the liquid into a glass. Add some sugar and drink it very quickly.' She knocked back her head with a laugh and sucked in the air with her teeth, miming the action of drinking such a mixture. I thought she was teasing, but the village doctor confirmed that it was, indeed, a commonly known 'cure' in the area.

He said a patient had once informed him that this horse dung cure was very dangerous because it gave one spots on the lungs. The patient explained that his father had taken this treatment many times in his life although it had never really worked. When he had eventually been sent to hospital for a chest X-ray, he had seen black spots on his lungs with his own eyes. He believed them to be residues from all the horse dung cures he had taken, but he had not dared to tell the hospital doctor about it at the time.

Other cures that the villagers used, such as plantain *(Plantago)* for burns and stinging nettles as a cure for rheumatism, were familiar from western folk medicine. One of the nurses at the local dispensary used the root of a plant called *luminărica-pământului*, or the willow gentian (*Gentiana asclepiadea:* gentian of Asclepius, the Greek god of healing), to cure liver complaints. Known to Dioscorides, the first-century AD Greek physician and author of the great herbal *De Materia Medica*, it was used by him to heal poisonous bites, internal bruising, stomach complaints and convulsions. According to Pliny, the name gentian derives from Gentius, King of Illyria, who lived in the second century BC and was the first to discover the medicinal properties of the plant against plague. So perhaps the Illyrian miners, brought to Transylvania by the Romans to mine gold and silver in nearby valleys, introduced knowledge of the plant to the area.

During my stays in the Apuseni, almost the only task to which I was allowed to contribute was haymaking, and even then, as a foreign townie, they only let me rake up the hay into small piles in the fields – protecting me from the more laborious work of pitching it up onto the stack. Haystack spotting is a richly rewarding game in Transylvania as there are so many techniques and varieties. In the Apuseni, the method was to build up a stack around a slender pole of young spruce. In Maramureş, hay is hung out to dry over specially erected wooden hurdles like clothes on a clothes horse before being made into haystacks. Most spectacular of all are the haystacks around Sarmizegetusa, kept high and dry in specially cultivated trees.

Haymaking was a crucial time of the year. In the mountains, the weather was extremely changeable and a prolonged period of rain during the summer months could be disastrous. One literally had to make hay while the sun shone. It was essential to see the animals through the winter. If there was insufficient hay, animals would have to be sold or killed. The work was arduous on the sloping meadows as everything was carried out on a steep gradient. It was often backbreaking but families and neighbours helped each other out, and there was usually a great sense of camaraderie. Many jokes and stories were shared during the long hours of work. The grass was cut with a scythe, which was tough work but nonetheless satisfying. There was also something profoundly graceful about the movements of a skilled person working a field with the rhythmical swish of the scythe against the grass. The traditional methods still used here meant that there was a breathtaking richness of plant and animal life. One only had to step into a field to count flowers such as harebells and metre-tall bellflowers, dark mullein, tiny wild strawberries, Carthusian pinks, globe flowers, and yellow and pink scabious, as well as many different species of grass.

One afternoon in the Apuseni, we were haymaking in

Right: *Scything in the mist. Traditional methods mean that there is a rich variety of plant and animal life in the hay meadows.*
Following page, left and right: *Washing day. Traditional washing machines. These eco-friendly machines channel river water into a tub where the woollen blankets are pummelled and cleaned by the force of the churning water. There is no need to use any soap.*

the field nearest the house: Ileana, her two young daughters and two neighbours Anca and Maria. At the end of the day, Anca and I began to carry the hayricks to the barn, supporting them on two poles, like sedan-chair carriers. I forgot about the ditch in the middle of the field and fell really hard into it with my right foot. Anca immediately threw her end of the poles on the ground and doubled up with laughter, shouting to Ileana and her daughters, who were standing by the barn ready to pitch the hay into the loft, to come and look at me in the ditch. I climbed out, and we continued to the barn. As soon as we had deposited the stack there, Anca came rushing round to hug and kiss me, putting her arms round my waist because she was very small, '*Oh, dragă mea, draguţa*' (O my love, my little love). The tears of laughter streamed down her face as she relived the moment of my fall. None of them asked if I had hurt myself. The fact that I had got up and continued to walk was proof enough that all was well.

Their good humour and ability to make light of misfortune shone out in lives that were unremittingly hard. For me, haymaking and milking cows in this

Right: *Carrying water home in the snow. Many houses do not have running water, which must be fetched from a well or spring.*

beautiful landscape was an exciting piece of time travel, a bit of make-belief in a rural idyll that was not idyllic for the people who had to live here. For women like Ileana, these jobs represented just a fraction of the relentless drudgery that cracked their hands and lined their faces prematurely. In addition to her household and farmyard duties, performed with no running water and only a small tin wood-burning stove, she earned a little extra income cleaning at the small factory which produced wooden staves, where her husband worked part-time. For this, he brought home the equivalent of about £50 each month. As this was their only source of income, it was essential that the family was almost self-sufficient in terms of food at least.

Right up to the present, the majority of men in this area used traditional scythes (scything is usually a man's job), their handles made out of ashwood because it is light and flexible. Recently, motorised scythes were used in the area for the first time by a large number of younger men. They estimated that it was seven times quicker to cut a field with them. The only problem is that any area of rocky ground has to be avoided in case the motor is damaged. This means that rocky areas are in danger of being abandoned, which would result in a loss of biodiversity. The converse danger to abandoning the environment and letting it go completely wild is deforestation and overgrazing by domestic animals, which means that the wild animals of the forest would lose their habitat and their food supplies.

One recent initiative to help local people appreciate the economic advantages of keeping traditionally managed grassland is a scheme to harvest arnica flowers. A team from the University of Agricultural Sciences and Veterinary Medicine at Cluj, with funding from the World Wildlife Fund and the British Darwin Initiative, has taught local people how to pick arnica in a sustainable way, set up a drying centre, and negotiate contracts directly with pharmaceutical companies. Romania and Spain are the main sources in Europe for arnica, which is in high demand for the treatment of sprains, bruises and rheumatic complaints. Elsewhere, arnica is in decline, and it will only continue to thrive in Romania if the alpine meadows continue to be managed in a traditional way and the plants are not overharvested.

Excellent schemes such as the arnica project were by necessity only on a small scale and dependent on foreign funding. Each year, the villagers find their way of life under threat, either from the increasing pressures to acquire material goods, to change their traditional wooden houses for larger concrete models that are perceived as better, or from tourism. One of the problems of recent years has been the restitution of private forest confiscated under Communism. In some cases, people have received only small parcels of forest, which they have then sold off or cleared for short-term profit or have not managed well through a lack of knowledge and experience. There have been a number of scandals caused by the lack of any means to prosecute those who have carried out illegal logging, both because of inadequate funds and infrastructure and because of corruption at many levels of society.

Mircea was worried about his environment being ruined. A cave that had been discovered just a few years ago had already been wrecked: stalagmites had been broken off and taken away as souvenirs and graffiti now decorated the interior. The past 30 years had been difficult, he said, but since the revolution life had been disastrous. He thought that democracy had brought a terrible sort of freedom to Romania by which people felt free to do anything and take whatever they wanted; no one seemed to have a sense of responsibility any more.

Visitors to the Apuseni saw everything in touristic terms, as something pretty, to be enjoyed for a moment like a programme on television – then switched over, or off. For the villagers, every tree, plant and field was of significance and of value to them. It was their life, their ancestors' lives; but as for their children's lives, they were unsure what would happen to them.

There is a story told in this valley about how one of the highest mountains in the area got its name – Hen Mountain. It is rich in local detail and still has resonance today:

Once upon a time, so long ago that even an old man from the village no longer remembers it, the summit of Hen Mountain was adorned with a glittering palace where a good fairy lived. The fairy had a hen that laid three golden eggs every day. When the fairy was in a good mood, each young married couple in the area would receive a golden egg as a gift.

One fine day, three local boys from a village at the foot of the mountain decided to steal the hen because they were very poor. With great cunning, they dressed up as poor local women and succeeded in breaking into the palace and stealing the hen and a basket of golden eggs. But on their way down the mountain, they got lost in the surrounding forest and the hen began to cry out. The guards were alerted and sounded a tulnic, *or alpine horn, in alarm. Troops of riders went after the thieves but could not find them. The basket with the golden eggs turned over and the eggs rolled from the top of the mountain into the Arieş [pronounced Ariesh] Valley. From that day on, the banks of the River Arieş were sprinkled with gold. The hen was trapped in a cave in the nearby mountains, and its gold is now hidden in the cave's innermost depths. And the good fairy, angry that the local people should rob her, ordered the palace to be demolished and left for another mountain. Boys and girls climb up to the top of the mountain nowadays in vain, for no one will ever give them a golden egg.*

As the legend suggests, nothing but traces of gold can now be found in the Arieş Valley, and until the 1970s particles of gold were caught in the River Arieş and its tributaries by nailing sheep fleeces to boards and laying them in water during the spring thaw. It has been suggested that it was this method of finding gold that gave rise to the legend of the Golden Fleece. It is a pleasing coincidence that the River Arieş bears the same name as the Latin for ram.

To the south of this valley are the Munţi Metaliferi or Metal-Bearing Mountains, where gold, silver and mercury have been mined for thousands of years. In the early 1860s, Charles Boner recalled how, while riding through a place he calls Verespatak in the Apuseni, he heard the sound of hammers resounding among the rocks: 'Presently, high above us, two men emerged from a long-deserted gallery; they were seeking for gold where some Roman soldier had begun and then ceased his toil ...' Verespatak, which means Red Creek in Hungarian, is now known by its Romanian name, Roşia Montana, meaning 'Red Mountain'. The place names in both languages are inspired by the red colour of the earth and water caused by their rich mineral deposits, particularly iron. The Saxons, ever alert to money-making possibilities, bluntly called it Goldbach or Gold Stream.

The Transylvanian Saxons were famous for their craftsmanship in silver and gold, and found work at various courts throughout Europe. In the medieval period, surnames were not necessarily fixed and passed on from one generation to another as they are now; when people moved from their place of birth, they were often known by the name of the place they came from. Thus it is known that there was a Hans Sybenbürger in Vienna at the beginning of the fifteenth century, a Lucas Sybenbürger at the court of Maximilian I in the sixteenth century, and the master goldsmith Georg Siebenbürger worked at Augsburg between 1573 and 1617.

Saxon craftsmen were especially renowned for their work in filigreed enamel, which appears in foreign inventories under the name 'modo transilvano',

Right: *Shoeing a horse. Transylvania is rich in metals and many made their living from mining and metalwork. The Saxons were famous for their craftsmanship in gold while gypsies still make horseshoe nails and also work in copper.*

although the technique was originally an import from north-eastern Italy. The Saxons did not create work for export or tribute alone, of course, and there was demand from the Romanian landowning classes in Wallachia and Moldavia, who commissioned ecclesiastical objects and frames for icons. Gypsies also bought silver and gold. Silver medallions survive that show gypsy princes outside their tents, with their names inscribed below. For the nomadic gypsies, silver cups, jugs, vases and buckle belts represented their material wealth and were treated with religious devotion, passed down from generation to generation and only pawned at times of dire distress.

The craftsmen also excelled in the jewellery that decorated Saxon and Hungarian national costumes, such as the elaborate pins for tying the women's headgear and for fastening parts of their dresses. By the end of the eighteenth century, however, the wares of Viennese workshops, producing work on a more industrial basis, began to flood the market, and the Transylvanian craftsmen of the nineteenth century tended to use Viennese models rather than develop work in their native style.

***Left:** The Dacian fortress at Blidaru, one of the last refuges of the Dacians against the Romans. The Emperor Trajan is said to have returned to Rome with vast quantities of gold and silver from Transylvania.*

To the Romans, the mines at Roşia Montana were known as Alburnus Major, colonised by Illyrian miners who had experience of working in the vast mines of Dalmatia. They are among the best preserved and most extensive of any in the world. The Roman galleries can still be visited, with niches cut into the rock where the miners kept their oil lamps. Until they were lost to the Romans in 270 AD, the Alburnus Major mines were the second most important source of gold for the Romans after north-west Spain. In addition to the mines, several temples, baths, burial sites and a mausoleum have also been discovered. Some 25 wax tablets have been found in the area, mainly recording contracts between the Roman state and private investors who rented out the mines to contract workers. The contracts were thrilling finds, helping historians reassess the way in which labour was used in Roman times. One contract, for example, concerns a freeborn local miner, demonstrating how the assumption that only slaves and prisoners worked in the mines can be exaggerated.

Now the whole area – some 43 square kilometres, including four mountains – is in danger of being blown up and all traces of the ancient mines blasted away by a Canadian mining company, which plans to use a cyanide lake in the extraction process. This means that the entire valley will be transformed into four open-pit mines and the neighbouring valley will have a cyanide storage lake, six square kilometres with a dam 180 metres high.

The old legend seems tragically apposite. Once the gold is extracted, there will be little left for the local people except a devastated landscape. Because the rich seams of gold and silver have been worked out over the centuries (in addition to the Roman galleries, there are traces of medieval mines, as well as those dating from the seventeenth to nineteenth centuries), any remaining metal is widely dispersed in tiny amounts. This is why the mining company plans to blast the landscape to pieces, exposing the metals to cyanide so that it will separate from the rock. The fight for Roşia Montana's future has been bitter and protracted. In a battle that has been fought since 1999 and is still not resolved at the time of writing, the local – extremely poor – community has been divided between those who understandably wish to take the money offered by the company to vacate their houses and build new lives elsewhere and those who, equally understandably, refuse to leave their ancestral homes and abandon the graves of their forebears. Each side has found vociferous support. The Romanian government is broadly in favour of the scheme and supports the company's project. On the other side are international environmentalist groups. The consequences of cyanide extraction have already been experienced at first-hand. In 1999, thanks to lax safety regulations at an Australian goldmining company in the north of Romania, as much as 100,000 cubic metres of waste water contaminated with cyanide poured into the River Tisza, polluting the major river systems of Central Europe, including the Danube. It also contaminated the well water of the local population, who were not informed of what had happened for several days after the event and so continued to drink contaminated water.

Transylvania has long been exploited for its gold. The Emperor Trajan is said to have brought back vast quantities of precious metals following the Dacian campaigns of 101–2 and 105–6 AD. A sixth-century Byzantine writer, John the Lydian, quoting from *Getica*, the lost work of Trajan's doctor Criton, who accompanied the emperor on the campaigns, tells us that he brought back more than 200,000 kilos of gold, double the amount in silver and countless valuable cups and vases. These figures were no doubt much exaggerated, but provide an indication of the value of the Dacian gold and silver mines to the Romans. The spoils of the Dacian War certainly contributed to the building of Trajan's Forum in Rome and Trajan's Column, which records in cartoon detail the history of the campaigns. An exact replica of the column stands in the Victoria and Albert Museum, London, and also in the National History Museum in Bucharest, where, most usefully, it has been cut into sections so that the visitor can view the detailed scenes at eye-level. Although the column celebrates the defeat of the Dacians, the Romanians regard it with pride, as though it were proof of their lineage. A sentimental anecdote is still repeated about a Romanian peasant who walked all the way to Rome to see his ancestors on Trajan's Column and was amazed to see that they were dressed in exactly the same clothes as he was wearing.

John the Lydian's comment about cups and vases may have been a reference to the Dacian king Decebal's fabled treasure. The Roman historian Cassius Dio mentions it in his gripping account of the campaigns (which includes secret messages written inside mushrooms, poison, the heroic story of the centurion Longinus, fantastic feats of engineering and buried treasure). He tells how Decebal diverted a river and buried fantastic quantities of treasure underneath the bed. He then set the river back on its original course and had the engineers who had helped him killed so that they would not betray his secret. In the end, Decebal committed suicide rather than let the Romans capture him, and the whereabouts of the treasure was eventually revealed to the Romans by one of his own men.

The myth of buried treasure is a potent one, and many still believe that more of Decebal's gold is hidden in the forests around his former stronghold. Illegal gold-diggers (who can be violent if disturbed in their activities) frequently find their efforts worthwhile. While out with one of the local park rangers one day in the Orăştie Mountains, I met a man who claimed to know someone who had in his possession two ancient tablets containing what he thought were Dacian inscriptions. The man kept them secret – quite plausibly – because he was afraid to hand them to the authorities in case they were stolen and possibly smuggled out of the country. My informant said he would have gladly taken me to see them, but as I was with a park ranger, and therefore a state official, he was not able to do so on this occasion. It was tantalising and extremely tempting to look at the tablets, but if I saw the inscriptions I would be compromised, although hopefully not forced to pay the price of Decebal's engineers.

Many grandiose claims were made during the Communist period about the level of civilisation attained by the Dacians, but although some conclusions from archaeological excavations might be controversial, the setting of the Dacian settlements in the Orăştie

Mountains south of Hunedoara is indisputably magnificent. Accessible only on unmade roads or on foot, the fortified settlement at Lunca Grădiştii – built at a height of 1,000 metres – is called Sarmizegetusa Regia. It is said to be the capital of Decebal's mountain kingdom and the site of his last desperate stand against the Romans. It is certainly a commanding place, looking out in a sweeping arc to the Dacian fortresses dotted around rocky outcrops of the surrounding mountains. When the Romans conquered it, they built their own fortress settlement on top of the devastated remains, but excavations have revealed the Dacian city beneath, including a sacred area with a series of sanctuaries and an altar, thought to function as a sundial.

Part of the charm of this site now is its remoteness and neglect. There is just one dented information board, and the extensive walls – Roman with reused Dacian stones – are covered in undergrowth. The only refreshment available is from a spring, guarded by salamanders that slither away into the moss when disturbed. The delicious water contains traces of silver.

The site of the Dacian citadel and of the Roman colony

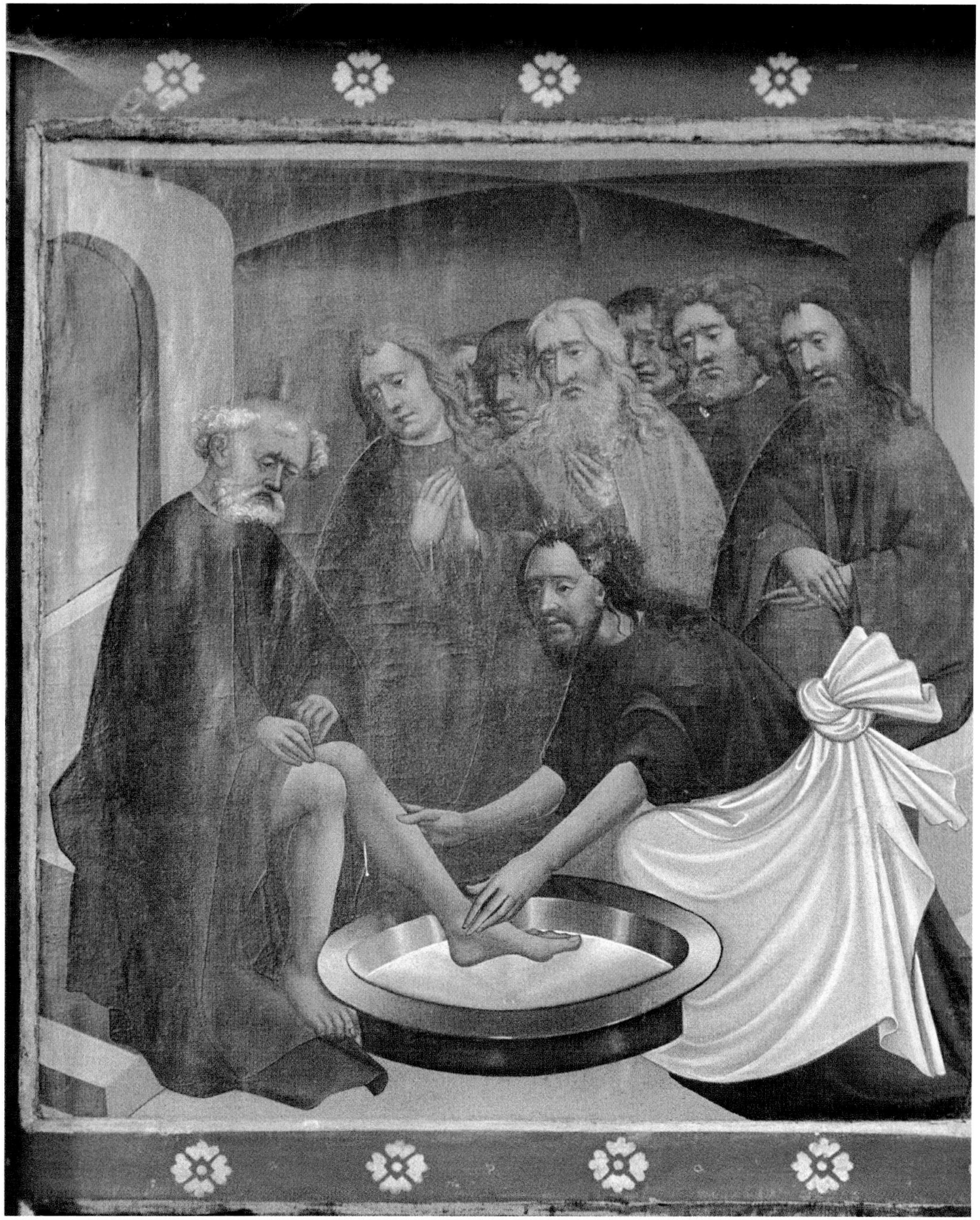

Right: *Altar panel at Prejmer. The Saxons imagined Jesus washing the disciples' feet in a huge golden basin. Transylvanian gold is still richly prized.*

of Ulpia Traiana Sarmizegetuza in the valley below is of great political importance to the Romanians, for the 'Transylvanian Question' – which nation, the Hungarian or Romanian, has the better claim to the land – lingers to this day. In the simplest terms, Romanians claim to be descended from Romans and Dacians who intermarried during the time that Dacia was colonised between 107 and 271 AD. After the Emperor Aurelian moved the Roman troops south of the Danube because of the threat from the Goths, the Daco-Romans stayed on in the mountains. The Magyars (Hungarians) settled in Transylvania during the ninth century. The Hungarians claim that Aurelian took all colonists with him and left the region deserted. The Romanians, they say, are descended from the Vlachs, a pastoral people originating from Macedonia and Albania, who spoke a form of low-Latin. These people moved into Transylvania at some point during the thirteenth century, long after the Magyars had established themselves there.

There is no doubt that Romanian and Vlach are closely related languages, and it is surely significant that both peoples in the past were called Vlachs or Wallachs (hence Wallachia). Romanians, however, argue that the Vlachs spread south from Dacia into the Balkans, or that the southern Vlachs are descended from those Daco-Romans who did evacuate south of the Danube with Aurelian. It could also be argued that as the Vlachs were a nomadic, pastoral people, it is possible that a branch could well have settled in the Carpathians before the ninth century. Whatever the truth may be, the Hungarians had established dominance in the region by the tenth century, and Transylvania became part of the Kingdom of Hungary.

When Transylvania came under Habsburg rule in 1691, the existing privileges of the three nations were confirmed, although all legislation now had to be sanctioned by the Habsburg emperor. The Romanians remained excluded. Their long struggle for recognition essentially began in the eighteenth century with the establishment in Transylvania of a Greco-Catholic or Uniate Church as it is also known. Ironically, this was an attempt by the Austrians to expand the influence of the Catholic Church in those parts of their empire where there was an Orthodox majority. In the Uniate Church, the ritual of the Orthodox service remained exactly the same except in three aspects: the Uniates were to recognise the Pope as the head of the Church; they were

Right: *The extraordinary church of Densuş, a tiny Orthodox church built out of pieces of Roman masonry. Large stone lions perch uneasily on the roof.*

to use unleavened bread during the mass and they were to accept the 'Filioque' clause, by which they acknowledged that the Holy Spirit proceeded from the Father and the Son rather than just from the Father. In return for their acceptance, the Uniates received certain privileges, the most important of which proved the establishment of schools where pupils were taught in the Romanian language. Until this time there had been almost no provision for teaching Romanians in their own language, even at elementary level.

Some promising students received funds to complete their studies in Rome and Vienna. A class of educated Romanians emerged which began to struggle for the political recognition of ethnic Romanians in Transylvania. One way in which they sought to establish the Romanian claim was to stress the Latin nature of the language and to emphasise their Roman origins by claiming descent from the Romans who conquered Dacia. For the Romanians, the Latin origin of their language was their trump card; through their language, they claimed lineage from an ancient civilised people. Roman Dacia, however, like any other colony, would have been populated by a diverse mixture of people from all over the empire – from Syria in the East to Britain in the West. (A Dacian cohort defended Hadrian's Wall in Britain, just as British soldiers were present in Dacia.) The fact that very few pure, unadulterated Romans would have settled in Transylvania unsurprisingly never entered the debate.

The idea that the Romanians may be descended from the Dacians, the native tribe conquered by Trajan and whose capital was in Transylvania, only began to gain ground in the second half of the nineteenth century. The Communists took up this version of the Romanian people's origins with enthusiasm. They were attracted to the idea that Romanians were descended from native Dacians rather than the imperialist Romans.

If any area of Transylvania could be described as its 'cradle', then it is the region around Sarmizegetusa. It is also significant for Saxon history, as Orăştie (Broos), the nearest town to the Dacian fortresses, marks the original western boundary of the Saxon territory. Further south, the Retezat ('Cut Off') Mountains are so-called because of the shape of the highest peak in their range, which looks like the sliced-off top of an egg. They also give the impression of being cut off from the rest of the world. In the last ice age, the whole area was an island on which, because of its limited size, a breed of dwarf dinosaurs evolved, the largest of which was a herbivore eight metres long and the smallest a carnivore only 60 centimetres in length. A number of duck-billed dinosaurs also lived on the island, and about 80 dinosaur eggs have been found in nests in river beds.

The presence of ancient life is felt strongly here. The land seems to be bursting with it. For Auguste de Gérando, who married into the Hungarian aristocracy and published a book about Transylvania in the mid-nineteenth century, memories seemed to rise up from this particular region with each step and transported him ceaselessly from one period to another. In a valley near to where the dinosaur eggs were found, a curious church at Densuş is the architectural embodiment of this broken mosaic of people and memory. A tiny Orthodox church, it is built out of pieces of Roman masonry in what now seems to be a random way. Roman columns without any architectural function are embedded into the side of the wall. Large stone lions perch uneasily on the roof slightly askew and out of scale with their surroundings. Now thought to date from the twelfth century, the church has withstood so many assaults and been patched up so many times that it is hard to make sense of it. The Roman masonry may have once adorned a Roman villa in the neighbouring fields or been transported here from nearby Ulpia Traiana Sarmizegetusa, the town that Trajan's army made their capital.

One plausible theory is that the church was a Roman mausoleum or was constructed out of the elements of one. Evidence that it was built in honour of Longinus, a leader of the Roman army who took poison when taken prisoner by the Dacian King Decebal, comes from the fact that the present altar table is made out of a Roman memorial stone dedicated to someone called Longinus.

The Romans may have exploited Transylvania for its precious metals, but it also has other resources that have provided rich pickings. Much of the land is covered in forest, and during the nineteenth century huge tracts of it were cut down, especially during the period of railway building. In the foothills especially there was large-scale deforestation. Where trees were replanted, evergreen spruce and pine replaced areas where mixed deciduous forest had provided a rich habitat for many different species of plants and animals. This should, of course, be put in the context of European history as a whole, where more than 50 per cent of forest has been lost since the Second World War, the majority in the West. During Communism, Romanian forests were well managed in the main, although the lack of opportunity for massive private gain and a scarcity of resources were probably the main reasons why they were less intensively harvested than in the West. The outcome is that the mountains and forests of Transylvania contain one of the richest and most diverse areas in Europe for animal and plant life.

Romania suffers from a negative press in the West, where only those stories that confirm its position as the hellish, or joke, land of vampires and Dracula, orphans and Ceauşescu tend to be reported. The countryside that one imagines to have been bulldozed, polluted and urbanised into a Communist hell-hole of faceless concrete apartment blocks and North Korean style uniformity is often much less changed that of the West. One hears of the terrible pollution in Romania, yet there is great scope for organic farming enterprises, if only because no one has been able to afford pesticides for so long. After the revolution, private land was restored up to a limited number of hectares. Working small plots of land using modern farming methods was not economically viable for the majority of peasant landowners, who reverted to old methods of farming using traditional means. Decades of resentment against the Communist appropriation of private land burst out after the revolution, and many collective farms in Transylvania were smashed in fury. The derelict cooperative farms were left to rot. Agricultural experts and technicians found themselves out of a job, and the people reverted to pre-industrial farming methods on their smallholdings.

Ceauşescu succeeded in 'systematising' some villages, herding people from their homes in the country and rehousing them in ugly apartment blocks as part of a plan to divide Romania into a series of giant 'agro-industrial' centres. There was investment in outdated heavy industries, which resulted in air and water pollution – sulphur emissions and acid rain – that had a damaging effect on rivers and forests. But it is often forgotten that Romania has suffered far less from unsustainable development in the past century and lost a far smaller amount of its native flora and fauna than other parts of Europe. In addition to the wolves and bears – mammals that became extinct elsewhere in Europe hundreds of years ago – there are lynx in the forests, and the imperial eagle, Ural owl and corncrake can find breeding habitats that have disappeared in the West.

Romanian membership of the European Union is often presented as a threat. The expectation is that hundreds of thousands of migrant workers will flood the job markets of Western Europe, undermining the native workforce, claiming benefits, putting pressure on housing, and so on. By contrast, Romanians are worried that they are the ones who will suffer from exploitation in their own country. They are concerned that they will become the 'supermarket of Europe', and be flooded with cheap imported goods to the detriment of their own native products and industries. In the country, time and again, people were more likely to express concern about joining the EU than undiluted glee at the massive

gravy train they were about to board. 'They will only let us keep three pigs,' they would say. 'All our cows have to wear these ridiculous earrings' (the yellow plastic tags). 'We won't be allowed to make our plum brandy communally.' After suffering under one of the most repressive regimes in the Communist bloc, people feel genuine trepidation at submitting to what is seen as another Big Brother, and they are cynical about the benefits. In order to claim money for loans to develop tourism, for example, it is necessary to have money already, but for the large percentage of the population that lives at or just above subsistence levels, this can only be a dream.

While the old ways were dying out in the Transylvanian countryside, nothing better had yet replaced them, as the majority of the people were still too poor to supplement their lives with the comforts that

Left: *Planting potatoes. Romanians worry that, as members of the EU, their country will be flooded with cheap imports to the detriment of native products.*
Following page, left: *Selling barrels at the fair. Men from the Apuseni sell wooden barrels at markets in Maramureş some 100km away, travelling there by horse and cart.*
Following page, right: *The plum brandy still. The communal village still is under threat under EU law.*

the outside world could offer them. The annual Girl Fair was held every summer on the summit of Hen Mountain, where the hen with the golden eggs had once lived. As its name suggests, it was originally a place to find women. In the past, unmarried girls from the surrounding hills would go there with their families and whatever they had to offer in marriage, including animals and beehives. There they would set up camp, arranging themselves and their possessions outside their tents, waiting for the young men to arrive. The couples that got engaged at the fair often did not marry until the following year, when their shepherd suitors had returned to the villages with their flocks. In the past, shepherds were away not just in summer, as now, but throughout the winter, when they would take their flocks far south. This was presumably why the festival was held on top of a mountain, as the shepherds were living in the high summer pastures. It would have been a brave girl who set up her stall on Hen Mountain without being sure of a betrothal beforehand, but the fair was a practical solution to the fact that people lived in remote and scattered settlements and needed to find partners outside their immediate families.

Now the original purpose of the fair has died out. It has become a festival for popular (folk) music and a market for selling goods rather than girls. Although many of the villagers now have electricity and televisions, it still takes several hours by bus to get to the nearest town, and most people are so tied by their work and animals that they have no opportunity to travel. This means that most marriages in the village are between local families, and there is a high instance of families marrying cousins. According to the local doctor, this inbreeding naturally causes a number of health problems.

A fair at the remote settlement of Calineasă, held annually in July, had once been an occasion for people to settle grievances in whatever way they thought necessary, by words or sticks and stones. Almost anything was allowed, short of knives and murder. The fair's name, the *Târg de Dat*, was a pun; it could mean trading goods or punches. It was a means of ensuring that grudges did not fester and erupt into uncontrolled, private violence. The fair still takes place, on a much smaller scale than the Girl Fair, but people tend to go there now to buy tools for haymaking, and to eat, drink and dance, rather than to strike their neighbours. Its original function has died out. Perhaps the opportunity of shopping one's neighbour to the Securitate during Communist times had rendered it defunct.

At local fairs and markets, the villagers would often rate pieces of pottery produced for mass consumption more highly than the simple clay pots or wooden objects they had once made for themselves at home. They would say, 'Oh, there is someone over the hill who makes much better bowls or spoons with patterns on them. He sells them to tourists. They are much finer than these old things.' Yet their wooden implements, made as practical objects for the home and farm, had a purity of form and function that was beautiful. As soon as they started to be made self-consciously as 'folk' objects, they became simply kitsch ornaments of neither practical nor aesthetic merit. The one remaining potter in the area was a young man who still knew how to make traditional pots, but he had survived by diversifying and making much more 'fancy' goods. His line in grotesque caricatures was a great success, and he sold his pots at craft fairs and outlets all over Transylvania.

Mircea always wore the same pair of old trousers for work, winter or summer. They were made of thick grey and black tweed, baggy at the thigh and narrow from the calf down like jodphurs, which Ileana had woven for him many years ago. 'When I was a boy,' he said, 'women used to weave all their own cloth, and would gather at

Right: *Girl from Maramureş with her dowry. The Girl Fair on Hen Mountain was originally a place where young men and women from surrounding mountain settlements could meet and get engaged.*

each other's houses and spin and sew and tell stories and sing, and my father played the fiddle. Before I married Ileana, she would weave such nice things, and every time I went to visit her up that high mountain where she lived, I would bring away a bag of striped cloth she had made for me. By the time we got married I had so many of them, I couldn't count them all!'

Mircea and Ileana laughed together at the memory of that time.

'And we used to fill the pillows and mattresses with beech leaves,' he continued.

Ileana produced a pillow that she had made herself and filled with leaves from a beech tree. 'The leaves in pillows must be changed every month', she said, 'so that the pillow stays crisp and fresh.'

'They are much more healthy than feathers', Mircea added. 'Leaves are better for children's breathing.'

The pillowcase, though, was made out of a garish pink satin acquired at the local market.

They also agreed that linen worked by hand, which they still used for sheets, and blankets loosely woven in coarse wool were much better than anything one could buy in town. Yet times had changed. Although Ileana kept a homemade, foldaway loom and a distaff in a corner of her room, weaving was considered to take up too much time and labour when cheap imported fabrics from China could be bought at the monthly markets.

A woman who had left the village at the age of ten said that when she was young in the early 1960s, everyone in the village still wore traditional clothes (which for the girls meant white shirts with embroidery at the sleeves, black skirts and embroidered waistcoats): 'Mother made clothes for all of us 14 children on the loom. What work it was. Combing the wool and twisting the distaff and spinning and working the loom. We didn't have the money to buy better clothes.'

'Better clothes?' I asked. 'I would have thought the ones your mother made for you were of finer quality than the ones you can buy now in the shops.'

'Oh, yes. They were very well made by Mama. They lasted much longer than the ones you buy now.'

She had said 'better' because the town was better, she thought, than the countryside. Now hardly anyone in the village wore traditional costume every day although people wore elements of it, such as the heavy woollen trousers or the massive and beautifully worked leather belts that shepherds and wood-cutters wore in the forest. Old women occasionally wore embroidered shirts on feast days, but the majority bought fabrics and clothes at the market, which they considered to be 'fine', and saved their traditional clothes for a dance or festival.

Despite all these changes – some sudden like the motorised scythes, others gradual such as the disappearance of traditional costume – the villagers' lives were still closely bound together. Each member of the family contributed to its daily survival by milking the cows, watching the sheep, chopping wood, fetching water, making butter, lighting fires: endless chores that to people in towns belonged to another age. The families in the village also relied on each other; they needed one another to help bring in the hay, to lend tools, bread ovens, the use of a horse and cart, or to give shelter to a neighbour's cow. Yet, as they became more dependent on the town and its products, they became infinitely less close. How tightly was a man bound to his wife when every article of clothing he wore was made by her, every piece of linen carefully stitched for him; when every morsel of food and drink consumed was a product of that couple's own labour. This is not to paint a picture of unrelieved domestic harmony. Men drank and became aggressive and were sometimes violent – episodes about which the women usually said little.

A lack of sentimentality about the old and reverence for all that is large, new and shiny also applied

Left: *Dancers gather at the Prislop Pass every year for a celebrated music festival. The Communists approved of such displays, as long as there was no bawdiness.*

to taste in architecture. In the centre of the village where Mircea and Ileana lived, the eighteenth-century wooden church with its pointed 'witch's hat' spire was completely overshadowed by a concrete one, a kit church with factory-made mouldings. This juxtaposition of old wood and new concrete has become a depressingly familiar sight in many villages. The old churches, as much a natural part of their surroundings as the trees and fields around them, look isolated and vulnerable next to their giant neighbours. Many wooden churches have also undergone the indignity of having the oak shingles on their roofs replaced with shiny metal sheets. Depressingly, in a country with so much forest, the cost of restoring a roof with wooden shingles is far greater than covering it in metal sheeting, because the skilled craftsmen necessary for the job are now in short supply.

Previous page, left: *Ploughing in a typical Maramureş landscape. Note the tall oak-shingled spire of the church roof in the background.*
Previous page, right: *Sowing. In many places farming methods do not greatly differ from medieval times.*
Left: *A wooden church under construction. Although Transylvania is covered in forest, new churches are more likely to be built in concrete.*
Right: *Piles of hay waiting to be made into haystacks.*

Inside the wooden church, it was a pleasure to climb up to the musicians' gallery by a ladder, each rung worn away to a crescent in the middle, to get a better look at the faded wall paintings, and sit there in the dusty light enjoying the smell of wax and faded incense and the musty warmth of old wood. The church was too small for the present congregation and needed major repairs. In comparison, the new church cost relatively little to assemble and the villagers gave their labour for free. It seemed unbelievable that a concrete church would cost less than a wooden one when all the land here was covered in forest.

Although their communities were still isolated, the villagers' horizons had expanded immeasurably through television and education. Their children now often finished their schooling in the towns and returned with different myths, superstitions and ideas. Increasing numbers of people sought work abroad, although many fewer in these isolated mountain communities did so than in the Romanian population as a whole. Just as a man was no longer bound to his wife by the threads of cloth he wore on his back, so each year the close-knit psychology of the village unravelled a little more.

Many of the traditions and rituals of everyday life are dying out fast, superseded by an understandable desire to acquire western lifestyles and material goods. The incongruous sight of a farmer on a mobile phone sitting on a horse-drawn cart is not uncommon. This desire for material goods is all the more understandable when one remembers that for several years before the revolution only the most basic goods were obtainable and even they were in short supply. Everything from sugar to toothpaste was strictly rationed.

Despite the encroachments of the outside world, time was still a different concept here, measured by the light, the weather and the number of jobs to be done. It made no sense to live by time evenly distributed and conveniently divided into hours, minutes and seconds. The church bells rang when it was time to go to church; for all other purposes, the people measured their day and the work they did by the light and by the weather, which differed from day to day and from place to place, from down in the village to further up the valley. I stopped wearing a watch and let the shadows guide me. We spent hours watching the cows and sheep. I never felt bored, nor did I once have the desire to read a book or write a letter. It was as if the landscape absorbed us; we just sat there and became part of it. Taking the cow to market, watching the sheep, churning butter with Ileana, it occurred to me that the only place I was ever likely to observe this way of life again was in the illustrations of a medieval Book of Hours.

Left: *Sledging and skating on the frozen river at Ieud in 1979. It is rare now to see children wearing traditional costume every day.*

Chapter 4

Christmas – A World Turned Upside Down

A journey to Maramureş is always an adventure, but particularly so by public transport in mid-winter. Isolated by mountains even from the rest of Transylvania, Maramureş has long been of interest to anthropologists, for it has one of the richest surviving peasant traditions in Europe. Its position on the borders of other countries –with the Ukraine to the north, Slovakia in the north-west and Moldavia to the east – meant that Maramureş was open to a different set of artistic influences than historic Transylvania. (Although under Hungarian rule and absorbed into the Habsburg Empire at the same time as Transylvania, it was officially never part of Transylvania.) After the First World War, only one-third of historic Maramureş went to Romania. The rest, which had a majority Ukrainian population, was awarded to Czechoslovakia and is now part of the Ukraine.

One of the chief delights of the landscape is the sight of its distinctive wooden churches, their spires, covered in oak shingles, soaring up to a height of 45 metres. They are such an elegant and harmonious element of the countryside that they seem to be part of it, although the soaring spires or onion-shaped domes betray the urban influence of the Gothic and baroque styles of Saxon and Hungarian churches. Almost none date before 1717, when a Tatar invasion destroyed most of the buildings in the region.

Like the churches that seem to spring up organically out of the surrounding landscape, the churchyards too are living organisms and extensions of the sacred space. Fruit trees shelter the lovingly tended graves, which are decorated with cut garden flowers, while wild flowers are left to grow between the graves. On All Souls' Day, candles shine from every grave, commemorating the village's ancestors. Outside some churches there is still a 'table of the ancestors' where a feast is held to honour the dead. The Uniate or Greco-Catholic Church, suppressed under Communism, was reinstated after the revolution, and many of the churches now follow the Greco-Catholic rites once more. In some churchyards, such as the church on the hill at Ieud, the Stations of the Cross are positioned on the way up to the old wooden church. On several important feast days, services are held outside, the church being too small to accommodate the large number of people who attend. When I first visited Romania, I was perplexed by what I took to be bandstands in the grounds of churches. These elegant gazebos are in fact where the priest celebrates mass on important feast days.

Left: ***The wooden church on the right with its soaring wooden spire blends in magnificently with the landscape. The vast modern church on the left is rather more conspicuous.***

Following page, left: *Hanging out traditional woollen blankets and cloths to dry.*

Following page, right: *Walking on planks of wood to avoid the mud.*

In December 1997, on my first visit to Maramureş, the sight of these wooden churches soaring intermittently above the snowy landscape provided encouragement and a grateful diversion as the bus rattled precariously up and round and down a series of hairpin bends on a narrow, icy road surrounded by beech forests deep in snow. There was heating inside but all the windows frames were loose, and only the ice that had formed between the gaps provided insulation from the cold outside.

The bus finally stopped 30 kilometres south of the Ukrainian border in the little market town of Ocna Şugatag. An Englishman had invited me to the village where he was carrying out research and had recommended that I visit the local vet, who would be able to find someone to accompany me to the place where he was staying. It took a couple of hours, but eventually I was assigned to a woman with a smooth, red face who was returning to the same village after a morning visit to the market. She was wearing the traditional winter costume of the area: a thick white woollen jacket trimmed with black braid worn open over a white blouse and a stiffly pleated skirt which reached just above her knees.

On her feet she wore *opinci* (pronounced opinch), shoes of roughly sewn hide worn with wads of wool wrapped round her feet and calves that were secured with criss-crossed leather thongs. I had only ever seen such shoes before in children's illustrated histories of the Vikings and King Alfred the Great. No one in the Apuseni wore them any more. Ileana last wore *opinci* to school about 30 years ago: 'They were warm but not very comfortable. In the snow they were fun, because the soles were so flat and smooth that you could slide along in them. But once I slipped down the hill and crashed into a tree. I cut my head quite badly.' She still had the scar on her forehead.

In Maramureş, a great number of the country people who were setting back to their villages from the market were wearing them. Most of the men wore thick white woollen trousers, wide at the bottom, with matching white jackets and astrakhan hats sitting high on their heads. The road out of town was busy, with old Dacias (Romania's home-grown car) chugging impatiently behind horses and carts piled high with an assortment of animals, people and sacks. One or two sheep were on leads, trotting behind their new owners like faithful dogs.

My companion, with typical Romanian solicitude

towards strangers, insisted that she share the weight of my bag, even though she was carrying a load herself in a large striped woollen sack slung over her shoulder. Even with the weight shared, I was not looking forward to the walk, and I was relieved when she spotted someone she knew in a car, who gave us a lift to the crossroads. There was no chance of any vehicle making its way any further, for here the road dissolved into sludge. On either side ran treacherous-looking ditches, still full of ice from the previous night's frost. As we picked our way along the troughs of mud and water for the remaining couple of miles, my companion warbled, as the women seemed to do in that part of the world, in a dialect that was all but incomprehensible. She pointed out the features of the village – the pretty old wooden church and the new concrete one standing starkly next to it, looking as awkward and alien in its environment as its older companion looked a part of it.

Someone was coming out of the door of the old church, and I could not resist a quick look inside. The interiors of old Maramureş churches are often richly decorated, with a fascinating mixture of influences from both the Orthodox East and Catholic Slovakia and Poland, together with a homely originality that depicts the immediate world of the Romanian painters – its landscape and architecture, horses and carts, flowers and trees. Although now sadly muted by age and damp, when new these paintings – executed in a naive style on strips of hemp or linen – would have provided a joyful explosion of colour, bringing the Christian teachings to life for the illiterate congregation. Most of the surviving paintings date from the late eighteenth and early nineteenth centuries. There are wonderful elements of fantasy. At Budeşti, Alexandru Ponehalski painted a scene from paradise with a charming procession of wonky animals, which he must have taken from a pattern book, as it is hard to imagine that he ever saw a camel or elephant – let alone a satyr – during his peregrinations as a painter in the Carpathians in the 1780s. Flowers and stars form a rich decorative background to Radu Munteanu's paintings. His *Creation of the World* at Deseşti is particularly moving. God looks like a benevolent obstetrician performing a Caesarean as he plucks Eve out of the side of a sleeping Adam and gently cradles her. Unfortunately, with the exception of pictures of the Virgin Mary, any hint of sympathy towards women in the painter's scheme abruptly ends when Eve succumbs to the snake's tempting apple and Adam and Eve are expelled from paradise.

Considered ever after to be particularly susceptible to temptation, women had to endure moralising scenes at the back of the church where they were obliged to stand. In villages such as Poienile Izei, they were treated to an unpleasant cartoon of devils torturing women in various ways: warning those among them who stayed in bed rather than listening to the priest, or who bewitched people or put charms on cows to prevent them giving milk. It was not only women who risked terrible punishments on the Day of Judgement. In this church, Jews, Turks, Tatars, Arabs and Gypsies were condemned to hell, while in Deseşti, the French and Germans joined the Turks and Tatars on the road to eternal damnation.

Although relegated to the back of the church, women formed a devoted congregation. If there were too many people to fit inside, they would huddle outside, their ears close to the walls, listening to the mass and intoning the responses. At Easter, women were more likely to fast completely for three days, forgoing all food and water so that they could take communion. During this time, they continued to go about their many arduous daily chores, looking after the household and animals and preparing the Easter feast.

Some of the richest traditions for celebrating both

Right: *Women outside church in Maramureş. The wooden churches are very small and often there is no room for everyone to fit inside. The men always stand at the front of the church and so the women sometimes sit outside.*

marriage and death survive in Maramureş, and it is here that the 'wedding of the dead' – the symbolic funeral that takes place when an unmarried man or woman dies – survives in its fullest form. For several decades the village where the Englishman was staying had been the subject of anthropological study, for even in this remote region its distance from the road meant that traditions had been preserved here in a way that was considered pure and isolated from too much contamination from the towns. There had been only a few collective farms in the area, largely because of the mountainous nature of the landscape; as in the Apuseni, everyone practised agriculture on a small scale at home. It was usual for each family to have a pig or two, some sheep, a cow and chickens, and to carefully tend a vegetable garden. A hay field was crucial if the animals were to survive the winter.

On the evening of my arrival, just after we had enjoyed delicious bean soup with some engaging children who lived in a neighbouring house to the Englishman, we heard a jangle of cowbells in the lane outside. It sounded not like the random clang of a bell round a cow's neck but as though dozens were being shaken together at once. 'Teodor!' shouted Viorica and she rushed out of the door. Viorica was a marvellous girl of about 12 years old. She was a paragon of a peasant girl, with rosy cheeks, fair hair and amused, intelligent eyes. She had the broadest smile and would put her hand on her hip in imitation of her mother when she needed to chastise the younger children or when proposing some scheme to us, which she did in a wonderful, teasing way. On my return home I sent the children a starfish and some shells because they had never seen the sea, and she wrote me the most beautiful letter I have ever received. Composed in rhyming couplets (as is all ritual verse in the region), it was full of vivid images of all the fields, hills and flowers that I had left behind.

Left: *Snowball fight. Many children now live with their grandparents because their parents work abroad.*

A moment later, Viorica returned from the yard with her brother Teodor, who was dressed in an extraordinary outfit. He had attached leather straps of cowbells round his body, covering his clothes almost entirely. Smaller belts of bells were wrapped round a large staff. A large sheepskin mask covered his face. Its teeth were dried beans, the shaggy eyebrows and moustache were horsehair, and it had a cockerel's beak for a nose. Teodor was taking the part of a devil and was on his way to a rehearsal for the mummers' play, which was to be performed between Christmas and New Year. We followed him out of the house and into night air that cut our faces with cold. The sky was so clear that not a patch of it was free of stars, and although we were now well behind the others who were carrying an oil lamp to light their jangling way, we could see clearly and our icy path glittered so much that it seemed the stars were reflected in it. We picked our slippery way along it, following the sound of laughter and cowbells.

We entered a house full of boys aged about 12 to 19 years. Bottles of plum brandy were circulating at the same time as a ragsheet containing 'dumb blonde' jokes. More shepherds and devils came in. Although each mask fulfilled a stereotype, such as the goat, the devil or the shepherd, each boy had added individual touches. One had sown a rabbit skin between the eyes of his devil mask to form a dark forehead, made eye sockets out of the rabbit's ears, and attached horns made of wire and bone bound in black wool, and a tongue of red leather. Another hung flashy little pictures of girls in bikinis, of the sort found in packets of bubblegum, from the cheeks of his shepherd mask. Then Death walked into the room, and the little girl of the house, who was standing by the fireplace, hid her face in her mother's apron. Death was tall, with a hunched back and a dark grey hooded cloak that stretched down to his feet. He wore a grey mask with floppy ears and a long snout. He looked part goat/part wolf, and his eyes were dark and hideously vacant. When he walked over to a stool by the fire, the little girl, still shielding her eyes with the apron, dragged her mother to the opposite corner of the room where her grandmother was sitting. These three were the only women present; Viorica and her sisters had stayed at home. The rehearsal was for a play called *Viflaim*, or Bethlehem, traditionally performed between Christmas and New Year outside the church. The play was introduced through the Greco-Catholic Church in the eighteenth century in an effort to introduce a more Christian element into the end-of-year celebrations, which were strongly pagan in form. But seeing the boys in their strange animal masks, it felt as though the pre-Christian element had not been repressed entirely, and it was altogether stranger than any Nativity play I had ever seen. The Communists suppressed the Uniate Church because of its allegiance to the Pope and connections to the West and the churches became Romanian Orthodox, but many of the region's customs, inherited from the Greco-Catholic tradition and deeply ingrained after 200 years, persisted.

The boys sitting on my right was 19, due to start his national service in the New Year. He was at the rehearsal to help test the younger boys' lines. When one of his friends came into the room, he called him over. His friend nodded in my direction without meeting my eyes, as a man does when he meets a woman here, but my self-assured neighbour told him, 'You should shake her hand. She's an English girl. It's all right.' The embarrassed-looking friend gave my hand the most peremptory of touches. Here was a scene straight out of Thomas Hardy's *Return of the Native*, as when the haughty Eustacia Vye had to promise one of the local mummers that he could kiss and hold her hand in return for letting her disguise herself in his costume. Holding a girl's hand here in Maramureş was presumably as impertinent and sensuous an action as it was in nineteenth-century Dorset. My confidence in the forbearance of Maramureşean manhood was a little premature, however, for towards the end of the rehearsal, to the delight of the assembled crowd, Death – emboldened by plum brandy and his disguise – made a grab at me as I walked through the door. But perhaps that is what Death inevitably always does.

It was only just after eight in the evening when we left the mummers' rehearsal, and we called on one of the village violinists on the way back. Climbing up the hill to his house, we saw flames in the distance and clouds of smoke smothering the thin, cold air. Against the orange of the fire was the black silhouette of a horse and cart. Men were unloading barrels and buckets oozing mushy plums and carrying them into the hut from which all the flames and smoke were issuing. This was the village distillery, where ţuică, or plum brandy, was being made, the country's most popular anaesthetic against hardship and cold weather. Throughout Romania, every rural village has its own distillery, usually a shed in someone's yard. The big copper stills are made by a traditional group of gypsies called the Kalderash (which means cauldron maker), who specialise in copper work. They can often be seen with their copper stills set out for sale along the sides of roads or at markets in the summer and early autumn.

Although the violinist's house was in darkness, there was a blue glow from the television, so we knocked on the window and called his name. The whole family had gone to bed because it was so cold, but the man insisted that we come in. His wife and daughter were lying in one of the beds and he was in the other, next to his sleeping son. They were watching a budget American Western. Although we protested, the violinist put huge slabs of pork pâté and hunks of bread before us.

Right: *Performance of 'Viflaim', or Bethlehem, enacted between Christmas and New Year outside the church.*
Following page, left: *Snow envelops the landscape but the traditional wooden houses and clothes are perfect insulators against the cold.*
Following page, right: *In winter, the wheels of carts are replaced by sleighs.*

After some village gossip had been exchanged, the violinist asked us about Northern Ireland because there had been a report of some violence there on the news and he found the idea of a religious war in Britain shocking. When we turned the conversation to music, he dutifully got out his violin and played some traditional wedding tunes. He was worried about a bad trend of gypsy music invading the area, with songs that were scandalously suggestive. This was the first time that I heard of *manele*, music that can best be described as oriental rap. The songs, strongly influenced by oriental dance music, are a hodgepodge of styles. *Manele* have now taken a firm hold in Romania and can be heard everywhere, despite the fact that no Romanian I have ever met – neither bus drivers, intellectuals nor peasant farmers – has ever admitted to liking or approving of them. Some of the tunes are extremely catchy, but the general consensus is that the lyrics are shocking on account of their salacious content and stupidity. They are universally despised as the music of the underclass, which usually means gypsy, and some national radio channels refuse to play them.

Even in this village, though, where the violinist did not play any western music and hated *manele*, changes were taking place. Once a week at the village bar the unmarried girls and boys danced to traditional music, but the musicians hooked up their violins to loud-speakers to achieve an authentic disco blare. This, however, was perhaps not such an innovation, for at the beginning of the twentieth century a certain Johannes Augustus Stroh, originally from Germany but then living and working in London, was inspired to fix a trumpet horn to a violin, thus magnifying the sound and giving birth to a new musical instrument: the horn, or trumpet, violin. In the early days of the gramophone, the sound produced by a conventional violin was not sufficiently directional for the early recording horns, used to focus the sound onto wax discs, to make effective recordings, and string instruments sounded thin and faint. Stroh's solution was to strip the violin of its body and attach a resonator to the bridge. This carried the vibration of the strings to a metal membrane and then amplified it through an attached horn.

Recording practice swiftly improved so that conventional violins could be used, but the curious new instrument seems to have entered folk culture via music halls and popular bands. It is not clear how or when it was adopted in Transylvania. As with so much else, its use has died out elsewhere, but it is still found in many parts of Romania – a modern, new-fangled instrument of its day, now being used to play traditional music and 'authentic' folk music.

When Hungarian composer and pianist Béla Bartók started to make recordings of peasant music in Transylvania at the beginning of the twentieth century, he regretted the fact that Franz Liszt had not had access to a phonograph when he had been collecting music in the 1880s, convinced that much had been lost in the preceding 20 years. Bartók discovered that the peasants he recorded demonstrated two contrasting tendencies. The first was to preserve their traditional village music, and the second was to imitate tunes they had heard from the towns, which they perceived as 'better'. The local musicians often adapted these urban tunes, transforming them into a hybrid. Musician and ethnomusicologist Ion Minoiu, collecting folk music on three field trips from 2001 to 2003, found a single musician who could play just one of the tunes that Bartók had collected: 'Jocul caprei la Crăciun' (The Dance of the Goat at Christmas). The player had never heard of Bartók.

Ion also observed a violinist in Maramureş playing conservative music in his own village, and yet when he went to play at a county folk festival he adopted a more flamboyant technique. Ceauşescu instigated large, organised 'folkloric spectacles', *Cântarea României* (The Singing of Romania), which continue to this day, supported enthusiastically by the tourism industry.

During Ceauşescu's regime, hours of television were devoted to programmes in which men and women in folk dress sang apparently traditional songs in 'Arcadian' settings. Hours of television and radio are still devoted to such shows of *muzică populară*, or folk music, with stout men and women of a certain age singing songs of youthful love which are no more authentic than hefty middle-aged English morris men performing dances that were intended for lithe young bachelors.

Ceauşescu made great efforts to industrialise Romania, investing in heavy and outmoded labour-intensive industries. He presided over the destruction of the historic centre of Bucharest and the 'systematisation' of many villages in the name of modernisation, but at the same time celebrated Romania's rich folk heritage. Having suppressed aristocratic and middle-class culture, the Communists allowed Romanian peasant traditions to survive as the nation's great inheritance. The celebration of old customs that supposedly dated back to antiquity provided a useful validation for the theory that the Romanians, as direct descendants of the Dacians and Romans, had a stronger claim to Transylvania than the Hungarians. Every village had its own cultural centre with small bands of dancers and musicians playing popular music. In most cases, the head of the cultural centre would instruct the local musicians on the 'correct' way to play. This led to a homogenisation of styles and the loss of traditional practices, such as the use of the guttural bass drone. In the Apuseni Mountains, troops of girls were taught how to play the *tulnic*, or alpine horn. Shepherds once used them as a primitive telegraph system and also to signal to the sheep that it was time to return to the fold. But nowadays, only women old enough to have taken part in the organised groups during Communist times play them, and it is almost unknown for male shepherds to use them.

The formation of popular music and dance troupes did not begin with the Communists. In the first few decades of the twentieth century and even earlier, middle-class enthusiasts began to encourage and collect all aspects of folk culture. Traditional costume also became fashionable among the upper classes, a trend encouraged by the British-born Queen Marie of Romania, who was often photographed in a suitably regal and Byzantine version of folk costume. As in England in the nineteenth century, there was a realisation that old traditions and customs were danger of disappearing with the homogenisation of culture that came with the industrial age.

Right: *Festival of the plough: originally a fertility rite, it was revived by a teacher during the 1960s.*

Dead or dying traditions were revived, such as the festival of the plough, an old fertility rite rescued by a Maramureş schoolteacher in the 1960s and now a well-established fixture on the festival calendar. I once found a cassette of folk music at the old Otopeni Airport in Bucharest during the days when it had only one small shop. The Romanian text on the inside cover explained what a glorious aspect of Romanian culture this music was. In English, it added that this type of music was 'enjoyed by peasants and a few intellectual crackpots in Bucharest'. I would have liked to have known who wrote this and in what circumstances the writer had come across the word 'crackpot'.

Intellectuals had been concerned about the disappearance of 'authentic' folk culture for more than a century. How far back did one have to look for it? When and where had a pure, unadulterated peasant culture ever existed? However quaint and timeless the lives and traditions of the people here may have seemed, no living culture is ever static, and folk culture, although conservative, is always subject to change and to outside influences. An old woman whom Ion Minoiu recorded in Oaş, a remote region west of Maramureş, was acclaimed in her village for her ability to sing long songs, yet she never sang the same one twice and would always improvise to suit her mood and audience. Maramureş is often talked about as a 'living museum' where traditions are preserved which have died out elsewhere, but this term, designed to captivate tourists, is a fallacious one. A living culture cannot be static, just like the old woman's songs or the interior of Frau Kräch's Saxon house.

***Left:** Woman with distaff. The large religious pictures round the wall suggest that she belongs to the Greco-Catholic or Uniate Church.*

Maramureş today is very different to the Maramureş I first visited in 1997 and bears even less resemblance to the region in the 1970s, still less to its pre-war self. The ethnic composition of pre-war Romanian Maramureş was entirely different to what it is now, with the Romanians then making up only 57.5 per cent of the population. Jews made up 20.6 per cent and Ukrainians 11.9 per cent, with Hungarians at 7 per cent and Germans 2 per cent. By 2002, Romanians represented 82 per cent of the population, and Jews were presumably included in the category 'Germans and other' at 0.39 per cent.

Many of the Maramureş Jews perished following the deportations of Jews from Hungarian-occupied Northern Transylvania in 1944: some 38,000 Maramureş Jews lost their lives. Little remains of this once large minority except for overgrown cemeteries and empty synagogues. In the large market town of Sighet, only one synagogue remains out of the 30 that served a population of some 15,000 before the war. Elie Wiesel, who was born in Sighet, tells the dreadful story of the 15,000 Jews of Sighet who disappeared in the space of just six weeks in *Night* (first published as *La Nuit*).

A mixture of rich local imagination and outside influence suffuses the history and culture of the region. Since the Second World War, men from Maramureş had commuted to local towns and also worked as seasonal labour in other parts of Romania, where they had a reputation as hard workers. Perhaps as a result of this long-standing tradition, a high proportion of young people have left the area to seek employment in the West; in some villages, few remain under the age 40. In the past, people were happy to acquire the outward trappings of contemporary life – fridges, big houses, televisions, cars – yet they conformed to the customs of the village by wearing traditional dress and engaging in its rituals, such as the dance, elaborate mummers' performances at Christmas, weddings and funerals. This is no longer the case, as increasing numbers of young people work abroad for longer periods of time and become removed both physically and mentally from the tight-knit psychology of the village. Their money is sent back to Romania to invest in building houses that bear

Right: *Wood and concrete churches. The new churches are much harder to keep warm and lack the intimacy of the wooden churches. On important festivals, many villagers prefer to use their ancestral church.*

little or no relation to the traditional architecture of the area. Old wooden houses are daily being dismantled, abandoned or sold to shrewd entrepreneurs from the West for as little as £100. Some may now be found in France, re-erected as 'traditional alpine houses' in smart ski resorts. While Maramureş is often fondly referred to as the 'Land of Wood', over the past 30 years concrete and double glazing have become the most popular building materials.

Even so, the first-time visitor today would feel themselves transported into another age, and in the 1990s Maramureş could not have felt more remote in time or space. Then most people, young and old, wore some form of traditional dress, even at the local disco. People who worked in towns and wore western dress at work would usually adopt traditional dress when they returned to their villages at the weekend and on holidays. Their clothes were an expression of their identity in both town and country and they adapted accordingly.

It is unlikely that so many people would have continued to wear traditional dress had it not been officially sanctioned. In a country so young and unsure of itself as Romania, displays of folk music and the wearing of folk dress were encouraged as a way of establishing a national identity from the earliest awakenings of national consciousness. Ethnic minorities within Romania also used it to make a political statement. The Saxons and, in particular, the ethnic Hungarians guarded their traditions all the more fiercely because they felt them threatened by the increasing Romanianisation of Transylvania. The wearing of national dress and the preservation of their own traditions and language became silent symbols of protest in an age when it was impossible to speak out against perceived injustices in other ways.

For romantically inclined westerners, the sight of traditional dress in areas such as Maramureş is thrillingly exotic. In *Three Years in Roumania*, the author comments:

... the common people are thus well and warmly clad in the national style. But alas for the picturesque! English importations are already making their way into larger towns and soon the handsome shepherd of the mountains will be reduced to the level, in outward appearance, at least, of the London cad or the Birmingham rough.

This paragraph was written in 1878; it was extraordinary that the everyday wearing of traditional dress had survived for more than a century longer than the anxious Victorian author anticipated.

Everyone in Maramureş aspired, of course, to large concrete houses rather than tumbledown wooden ones, or contemporary western fashion rather than traditional clothes, however much – like the people in the Apuseni – they acknowledged that their own homemade clothes were in some ways superior. No one could take them for fools. When the Englishman commented one day that 'only the poorest people in England wear shapeless, fake-leather jackets, and it's unbelievable that people here should want to wear them when they have such beautiful clothes of their own,' he was greeted with the swift reply: 'But we are the poorest people in Romania, so it's all right.'

It is easy to be moralistic about material goods and snobbish about fast food and shiny suits. It is possible to reject these things in the West, but for the villagers these were the only symbols of modernity and sophistication, of the fantasy world of American soaps, that they could afford. However much we might dislike the idea, we were much closer to this imaginary American paradise than they were, which perhaps was a part of our attraction to them. However many times we pointed out there were aspects of their lives that we thought were more desirable than ours, they could always reply, 'But

Right: *The entire side of the house stacked with logs. The small stoves in people's houses are surprisingly effective, especially in wooden houses.*

you can travel. We cannot afford to.' And for that there was no answer.

The fact was, of course, that in grinding poverty the peasants did not dream of Arcadia but of the world of the television soap opera. Ceauşescu's plan to raze the villages was, in part, the peasant's dream of clean and flashy modernity. Ceauşescu had, after all, ensured that his own village was one of the first to be modernised, not as a punishment but as a privilege. He had fancy street lamps and large flowerbeds constructed in the central streets; apartment blocks were built in place of the bulldozed houses, and he donated a large football stadium as an extra present for his birthplace.

Neither Communism nor capitalism cared for self-sufficiency but required people instead to be dependent on the values of the city. When the villagers stopped making their own clothes and baking their own bread, when they started to build houses out of concrete rather than out of the wood that surrounded them in the forests, they lost their independence and also something in their character. They became dependent on a world they did not know or understand well and which knew

Left: *Sawing wood in the snow. Life is particularly hard in the mountain settlements where the nearest shop or school may be several kilometres away.*

them only as numbers or statistics; the one system valued them for their productivity figures, the other in terms of their spending power.

Despite the all-encroaching consumerism, religion still infuses everyday life. In Maramureş, the villagers greet each other with '*Laudă-se Iisus*' (Praise Jesus), for which the response is '*În veci, Amin*' (Forever, Amen). During Easter, this becomes 'Christ has risen', with the response: 'It is true that he has risen.' These greetings are used specifically by members of the Uniate Church. The prayer for 'God to help you' – '*Dumnezeu să v-ajute*' – when a person takes leave of another, however, is used throughout Transylvania.

As in Maramureş, Christmas in the Apuseni is still a religious rather than a consumer festival. Early on Christmas Eve, Mircea fetched the tree he had cut from the forest. He sharpened the trunk to a point and stuck it in an iron stand. It stood lean and tall in his low-ceilinged house, and when Ileana put a paper crown on its top, which looked like the funny paper hats that used to adorn lamb chops, it brushed the ceiling. Oozing pine cones still clung to the tree, glazed by their frozen resin, but these were soon obscured by tinsel, baubles and sweets in shiny coloured paper suspended from strings. Their daughters balanced chocolate bars among the branches, giving the one labelled 'American Bar' pride of place in the centre of the tree.

The chocolates were the children's Christmas treats. It was not the custom to exchange gifts here except at weddings, when the exact amount of money or type of present was announced publicly. In a society so closely bound together, there was a perfectly understandable reason for this custom. Wedding gifts were a social obligation and given on the understanding that the recipients and their families would offer similar presents to those who gave the gifts on this occasion. If a person accepted a present outside this strict framework, it was feared that the giver might in some way exert a hold on the recipient, especially if there was no possibility of the gift being repaid. The dangers inherent in such transactions and the anxieties that arise from accepting a favour that cannot easily be repaid are demonstrated in many fairy stories, such as 'Rumpelstiltskin', 'Rapunzel' and 'Snow White and Rose Red'.

Yet in offering hospitality and in the giving of gifts that they had produced themselves, the Romanians are among the most spontaneously generous people. It is only in Romania that complete strangers have presented me with flowers for no apparent reason other than the pleasure in giving them. Walking high in the Carpathians one day with my father, we greeted a shepherd. Several hours later, we were a little alarmed to see this same figure running over the brow of a hill towards us, shouting out. He rushed up, gently bowed to kiss my hand, and presented me with an Edelweiss. A lonely bus driver once secured 11 of these flowers for me, a hopelessly romantic action as well as a reckless one for they are protected.

Such charming gestures were not restricted to forlorn shepherds and bus drivers. When walking near Sarmizegetusa one afternoon, a woman whom I had greeted on the path up to see a spectacular cave in the forest presented me with a huge bunch of flowers from her garden on my return. She wanted no payment, but simply wished to greet a stranger to her community. The giving of flowers has its particular rituals. When given to a living person, there should be an odd number of flowers, but if for the dead, the number must be even.

Late on Christmas Eve, the sound of drums and cymbals and the *taragot* announced that the carol singers were in Mircea's courtyard, demanding to be let in. The *taragot* is a reed instrument and a cross between a clarinet and a saxophone. Like the trumpet violin, it was a nineteenth-century invention adopted by dance bands for a short time and taken up with enthusiasm in Transylvania, where it has found its way into the folk repertoire while being virtually unknown elsewhere.

The carollers were all unmarried men in their late teens and early twenties, and their faces, already flushed with cold and drink, glowed bright red at the sudden rush of warmth when they entered the house. After they had sung their carols with great spirit but wholly off-key, they danced with all the unmarried girls in the room. Ileana danced with her younger brother Nicolai. It would not be seemly for a married woman to dance with a man who was not from her family and certainly not with one who was unmarried. My first partner had blue-green eyes under eyelashes that curled extravagantly, and a nose with an arrogant tilt to it. His voice was hoarse from a night full of smoke and rough drink, from all the shouting and singing, as Mircea's house was quite far down the valley and one of the last to be visited. Mircea gave the men *crampă* to drink. It tasted stronger than the plum brandy, if that were possible, and was made by roasting sugar on the fire, mixed with a little water, caraway seeds and pure alcohol. It was best served warm. Disconcertingly, Mircea kept his *crampă* in an old surgical spirits bottle. This was probably because of its label, which bore the legend 'Mona' and a photograph of a pouting woman with glossy chestnut hair wearing a scant and largely unbuttoned starched white nurse's uniform.

Because Ileana's two younger brothers were in the group of carollers, she allowed her daughters to follow them out into the snow to the neighbours' houses. They played their music through the fields, but when they got near the first house, everyone fell silent and did not start playing and singing until they were right outside the door, so as to surprise the householders, catching them off guard or perhaps asleep. This was an old and once widespread custom, which perhaps explains why many old English carols begin with the exhortation to 'Awake'.

As in the West, many Christmas customs seemed more closely related to pagan end-of-year celebrations such as the Roman Saturnalia, when the world was turned upside down and all laws suspended. As Bartók observed, a third of the text of Romanian carols had nothing at all to do with the Christian Christmas. In the past, the authorities had tried to ban carollers and mummers for being too violent and rowdy. In 1783 the deputy governor of Deva in Transylvania threatened to ban them unless the mayor and seven elders of the respective communities could guarantee that there would be no riots. In 1859, in his introduction to the first anthology of Romanian carols, Marienescu complained that the custom was in danger of dying out because police had been banning it to prevent breaches of the peace.

The carollers' next visit was to a house owned by people from the city of Oradea, who spent their holidays in the village. They wore fleeces, padded anoraks and spectacles, and ate from bakers' trays full of vanilla slices and fancy cakes, washed down with sweet Romanian 'şampanie'. They were welcoming and delighted with the music, but they all looked uncomfortable and ungainly when trying to dance in the traditional way, like old people trying to dance to pop music. The carol singers adopted a slightly distant, embarrassed look, which they also wore when they were talking to me in front of their friends. They looked suspicious of the vanilla slices, as they were of any unfamiliar food.

Everyone was laughing and telling jokes and singing, but the difference in tone between this party and village celebrations was evident. The villagers made jokes that were vulgar in a different way to the ones the town people told. It would have been unthinkable for village men to tell crude sexual jokes in front of unmarried women. In a mixed group, innuendo tended to be initiated by older married women, and then the older men might add their share. Younger men only told such jokes among themselves. Ileana's brothers shifted uneasily in their leather jackets and high sheepskin hats among the students in primary coloured salopettes and jackets. They felt out of their depth among people they

Right: *The man crossing the bridge wears traditional winter trousers made out of gleaming white wool, home-spun.*

considered to be more sophisticated and better educated than themselves and to whom they would automatically defer as 'Sir' or 'Madam'. The villagers were not wholly deferential to the town people. They would make fun of them in private and some of the younger men picked fights, but in a context such as this party, where they were unsure of the customs of strangers, they felt uneasy.

When it was time to leave the house, the musicians played while we danced down the wooden steps and through the fields until we stumbled in the deep crunch of the snow by the river. The frost stung my nose and cheeks and, exhilarated by the cold air and the pleasure of dancing, my happiness felt raw.

At the next house, which lay over a narrow bridge made out of loose and icy planks, Ileana was there, come to collect her daughters Dana and Jenica. She sat with the parents and their two daughters, who looked shy and hopeful. With which man did they most want to dance? Those carollers who had not managed to squeeze a place on a stool or divan slouched against the walls, which were painted half green and half white with a red stripe separating the colours. When the music began, the two girls were only too pleased to rush outside with the men who had asked them to dance, as conveniently there was no room to dance in the tiny house. After a few dances and a similar number of glasses of plum brandy, the men sang a couple of plaintive refrains from outside the window, and disappeared down the valley.

Carollers used to be paid in kind, given food and grain for their chickens as reward for their efforts. This grain was supposed to be lucky and ensure that the hens laid well. Nowadays they were given money. Most people thought this was a pity and spoke with nostalgia of the days when food and grain sufficed.

At church on Christmas morning, during a service that lasted for almost four hours, small groups of boys marched up to the iconstasis to be blessed by the priest. They were all about 12 years old and wore long white embroidered shirts, tied at the waist with big shepherd's belts. They wore paper hats woven out of multicoloured strips of paper and covered in polythene bags to protect them. The boys were in groups of three, representing the Magi. Each carried a cardboard sword, crescent-shaped like a Turk's, and wore cardboard breast plates and cuffs covered in shiny wrapping paper. A few of the groups had a fourth boy whose job it was to carry the Magi's guiding star on a stick.

One group of kings had come to Ileana's house on Christmas Eve, and had sung their carol without expression and without drawing breath. One boy with a particularly mournful face had teeth in such a bad state of decay that the bottom row was simply a series of points, like those in a cartoon drawing of a dog or a shark. Soon after they left, the dog barked in the yard and we saw another group of kings approaching the house. 'Oh, they are gypsies,' she exclaimed. 'We shouldn't let them in.'

'Oh, Ileana,' I said. 'I'd like to see them.'

Ileana looked doubtful. 'Well, if they come in, don't speak. If they know you are foreign they will want lots of money.' And she rubbed her fingers together as if she were sifting flour. A miserable looking group of three dark-skinned boys was half admitted, Ileana keeping the door open while they were there, not letting them past the threshold. 'That was terrible,' she said when they had recited their poem. 'Can't you do any better?'

The boys looked up at her uncertainly, then began to sing something else, but it petered out after a verse or two. 'That was no good either,' said Ileana, standing with her arms folded. 'You don't deserve anything.' They were so hopeless and looked so dejected that I felt I had to give them at least a chocolate bar and a few pence. They smiled, if nervously, for the first time but remained speechless.

'What do you say?' demanded Ileana.

***Left:** The three kings, a Christmas tradition throughout Transylvania. The boys sing a Christmas song from house to house and parade into church on Christmas morning.*

'Thank you,' they mumbled unsurely, now anxious to leave immediately to eat the chocolate and examine how much they had been given. Ileana followed them out into the yard to make sure that they did not take any of her chickens, and then shut the door as soon as she had counted them out of the gate.

'You mustn't give the gypsies anything,' she said sternly. 'If you do, there will be hundreds of them on my doorstep and we will never get rid of them.'

That Christmas was the first to be celebrated in the new concrete church, and it was so cold that it was blessed relief at those points in the service when we knelt down on the floor and so relieved the frozen soles of our feet. The men stood at the front, on the right hand of the church, their sheepskin hats piled up on the window ledges above them. At least there were seats now for those old women bent double with aching joints, who had to prop themselves up against the walls in the smaller old wooden church. Perhaps my brain froze with the cold, because the hours seemed to pass quite quickly, and just as the cold had become unbearably painful, the service ended.

The costumes of the goat boys who visited Ileana's house after Christmas were tame in comparison with the wild shamanistic-type masks of Maramureş. Their sketch involved two boys dressed in traditional shepherds' clothes, with white linen shirts and broad, patterned belts, and a 'goat' on a lead. The goat was a boy covered in a blanket, from the depths of which he controlled a wooden goat head with moving jaws, stuck onto a broom handle. The mummers gabbled their piece, and then the goat had fun running about and pretending to eat all the women. The first few lines began in a standard way and the refrain 'tsa, tsa, tsa, little goat, tsa' was the same as other such 'little goat' songs, but then it became progressively more strange, so that by the end it resembled more closely a spell or incantation:

A goat comes from the mountain
A white star on its forehead.
Tsa, tsa, tsa, little goat, tsa …
I will give you only beans.
Sit down on the ground so that the wind doesn't beat you
Watch out for the wolf behind you
Don't be scared it will eat you
Tsa, tsa, tsa, little goat, tsa
The trunk of the beech
The shade of the oak
Tsa, tsa, tsa, little goat, tsa.
I will give you only beans
This goat is from Bacau
Everything is on its back

Right: *The 18th-century wooden church at Ieud. Hardly any churches in Maramureş pre-date the Tatar invasion of 1717 when most were razed to the ground.*

Tsa, tsa, tsa, little goat, tsa …
This is a goat from Arieşeni
Pretty and fair
Won't you sell this goat to me?
Yes I will.
How much do you want for her?
Two million
That's too dear, don't you think?
Does it give milk?
Yes.
It kicks.
It gives me a kick
You gave the evil eye to my goat.
I will make three crosses on its head
So that three hairs of the devil will grow
And three on its hooves
May God give it to you.
May it give milk only to you.
Who has woken up my goat
Can only be the one with the music
Tsa, tsa, tsa, little goat tsa
I will give you only beans.

Mircea was proud of his piebald pig. On the last day of its life, he let it out of its sty. At first, it was reluctant to get out of bed, and he had to drag it up. As Mircea pushed the pig out, it bumped into the door and tottered down the steps into the courtyard like a small girl trying to walk in her mother's high heels. It crashed into me. Mircea kicked it in the flank with his rubber boots and gave a delighted, proudly proprietorial laugh as he looked at me.

'Do you like her?'

'How old is she?'

'Six months. We'll kill her tomorrow.' The pig bumped into the woodshed. Maybe it was short-sighted. Ileana came out of the house.

'What's that pig doing out here?' she screeched.

Mircea gave his slyboots smile as he shrugged his shoulders and kicked the pig back into the sty.

It is more usual to kill the pig before Christmas, but in Mircea's house it always happened before New Year. The day after the pig had been slaughtered, the cowshed was strangely silent. The two squealing black piglets that had lived in the corner by the door had been moved to the dead pig's more spacious sty, and their little pen was empty. The slaughter of the pig was an important

Left and right: *Preparing the pig; not one part is wasted. Cabbage stuffed with pork is a particular treat.*

occasion; it required a day of concentrated effort by the whole family so that every part of the pig could be put to good use. That evening we had pork soup. When I lowered my spoon into the bowl, it hit a large, hard lump, and I looked down to see a pig's ear, complete with a little black tuft of whiskers, wallowing just below the surface. I was prepared to eat most things (with the exception of the lard they smeared on hunks of bread and ate with raw onions), but I could not bring myself to bite into the pig's ear. I passed it over to Mircea and he ate it with pleasure, whiskers and all.

I had read somewhere that the man who came to butcher the pig said a prayer to it beforehand to ask forgiveness. When I asked Mircea, he laughed at the idea. But always eager to find some sort of solution to my questions, he said it was true that after the pig had been killed they ate the best parts – such as the heart, liver and fleshy bit at the back of the neck – and this was similar to the feast that was held for a dead person after his burial. The European Union has already decreed that pigs may no longer killed by the knife, which may well put an end to this particular tradition, as it will to many others, if and when it is enforced.

At New Year, there was a dance higher up the valley. It was held at the village bar, which adjoined the shop. Essentially these were two small wooden rooms sharing a covered veranda and a staircase up to them. Mircea did not go to the dance, preferring to stay at home and sleep. Married men rarely came. The dance was the province of unmarried boys and girls, and of the women who came to chaperone their daughters and gossip about who danced with whom.

When we arrived at about nine in the evening, it was already so crowded that people had spilled out onto the veranda to get some air or smoke cigarettes. We had to push our way through the door, as several bodies were leaning against it to make more room for the dancers. A handful of red-faced men were already being propped up by the bar counter, their eyes barely able to focus on the shelves full of vodka – every bottle a stomach-scraping brand.

Ileana's brother Marinel approached with a large old Coca-Cola bottle in his hand containing his home-brewed *crampă*. All sorts of homemade drinks were being handed round but no one seemed to mind. As the bottles were passed round, each person took a swig with the appropriate wishes for good luck, good health and a happy new year. But when Ileana's younger brother Nicolae offered the bottle to me, Marinel told him to wait and rushed off to the bar to get me a glass – he felt that a *domnişoară* (Miss) from the city could not swig straight from a bottle.

All the men at the dance, including the boys, wore grey or black sheepskin hats high on their heads. The musicians sat in a corner by the bar: there were two taragots and a drum with cymbals attached. A low bench ran round the room and was almost entirely taken up by older women, except for the bit nearest the bar, which was occupied by a few young men who had not yet mustered the necessary courage to ask any girls to dance. They sat unsmilingly with their arms folded, the local equivalent of looking cool. The married women sitting down wore headscarves to denote their status. They had layered sweaters and cardigans over their flowery knee-length skirts and dresses, and were clinging onto torches which they needed to light their way home after the dance. No one had a car so everyone wore thick tights, socks and stout boots, because most would have a few miles' walk home in the cold in the early hours of the morning. When the unmarried girls wanted to rest from dancing, they sat on the older women's knees, their girlfriends perched against their laps and the children perched on the friends' laps, so there were sometimes as many as four people stacked against each other.

It was hard to tell how old people were. Many women looked old in their fifties. People aged so rapidly that there seemed to be no gentle path from middle to old age. Marriage for women, on average at the age of 19, seemed to add instant years to their demeanour, and motherhood sent a girl tumbling into middle age. It was the same with the men, although because they often did not marry until their mid to late twenties, their youth had a few more years' grace.

Looking at the faces in the room, it seemed that the blood of only a few families had intermixed and remixed for generations, probably centuries. There were goggle eyes and cross eyes and a girl with eyes so wide apart you imagined she could see like an owl; silver teeth and gold teeth and broken noses badly mended. Of all the women in the room, Ileana was the most elegant. In her black skirt and blouse and the fox fur jacket she had made herself, she looked far more enticing than the younger girls in their jeans and shiny anoraks or potato-sack leather jackets. On the veranda, with her handsome dark-eyed brother, Ileana danced in her shabby, high-heeled suede boots, her only dance of the evening. Marinel shouted as he spun her round:

Fată ce joacă cu mine
Tare nea se ţine
Dar se poate şi ţinea
Că nu-i alta-n sat ca ea.
Girl who is dancing with me
The snow is holding fast
But she can hold fast to me
Because there's no one like her in the village.

His trousers were tucked into his calf-length boots like a Cossack, although the observation displeased him.

'No,' he said, 'like a Moţi.'

Some of the unspoken rules of the village were manifest at the dance. The married women chaperones watched keenly who danced with whom and how many times, and were acutely aware of the nuances of the loud shouts or calls known as *strigături*, four-line rhyming couplets which the men cried out during the dance. Few of the married women danced, and if they did it was only with a member of their own family: in Ileana's case with her brother. Even then, there was a sense that this was something not really done – the dance was for unmarried girls and boys, the place where 'men can know women', they said. It was considered bad form for a girl to turn down a dance with a boy – a public put-down – and a girl might find herself the butt of some mean *strigături* as a result.

Fata ce alege mult
Se mărită după mut
Că şi-a mea a tot ales
După mutălău a mers.
The girl who is too picky
Will marry a mute
Because my girl was always picky
And went after a big dumb lump.

Everyone took the dancing seriously. Women placed their hands on top of the men's shoulders, and the men held the women round the waist. As they danced, the men looked everywhere except at the women with whom they were dancing. Perhaps this was because they did not wish to seem too attached to one particular girl, especially with the eyes of the village's chaperones fixed beadily upon them. They preferred to keep their options open.

The noise in the room and tempo of the dances increased in proportion to the amount of drink consumed. The men began to dance more energetically and to call out the *strigături* more and more wildly.

Jucătoarea joacă bine
Şi mă-nvaţă şi pe mine
Că mă-nvaţă a jucă
Eu învăţ a săruta.
The dancing girl dances well
And she's also teaching me
She's teaching me how to dance
And I'm teaching her how to kiss.

These rhymes could be sweet or funny or suggestive, or a combination of all three. The next day, when I asked Marinel and a friend to write some down, they looked embarrassed. This was partly because of the content of the rhymes and partly because they were worried that they would spell words incorrectly, or that I would not be able to understand the dialect, or even that they had been asked to write at all. It was also difficult for them to write down lines which were part of the ritual of the dance, which may change according to the mood or situation, and which are only ever called out in the context of the dance with the rhythm of the music.

Many of the Moţi had had a limited education. It was difficult to get to school from remote settlements that were more or less impassable for several months of the year, even on foot, and it was not uncommon for children to walk several miles over the hills to reach their schools. With such difficulties and with the labour-intensive life that most people lived, sometimes without running water, it was not surprising that children were often thought to be more usefully employed at home than at school. Many adults in their fifties and older were barely literate, and even younger people often expressed embarrassment at not being able to write well.

At last, after much sucking in of breath and consultation with his friend, Marinel offered to write some down. His friend nudged and smirked as he pretended not to know the rest of the words to one or two rhymes I recalled from the dance. Marinel held his pen with the concentration of a child joining up his first letters, and was so impressed with his handwriting that he showed it round to everyone: 'And I haven't held a pen for more than a year,' he said. The verses were rich in dialect and contained some very specific words. 'Gozu', for example, is a dialect word for the mud you scrape off your boots at the front door.

In the basic dance, the dancers stomped their feet to the right and left, moving round slowly in a circle to the heavy beat of the drum. The man could add many other steps to this routine, such as scuffling his feet energetically while swaying slightly from side to side. Then, waving his hands in the air and snapping his fingers, he cried out, in time to the beat, the *strigături* with deafening interjections of 'Hoi, hoi, hoi-a, hoi!' The dancing pair circled round, the woman passing under the man's arm and then the man under the woman's. The dance could be taken at various speeds so the dancers could trip round slowly or whirl round until they felt faint. At the end of each dance, the man pressed his partner to him briefly or lingeringly, depending on his relationship with her or his audacity, and bowed his head, thanking her for the dance and wishing her good health and happiness.

Right: *Most horses are for work rather than pleasure.*

Câte mândr-n braţe am strâns
Toate după mine au plâns
Şi de-acum câte-oi mai strânge
Toate după mine-or plânge.
All the proud girls I held in my arms
They all cried after me
And from now on, all the women I'm going to hold
Are all going to cry after me.

It was a seven-kilometre walk back to Ileana's house and early morning cold dug right in. It felt as though great chunks were being gnawed out of our noses and cheeks. The river had frozen and the frost had crystallised all the trees and fields, so it was hard to tell whether the earth or the stars shone more brightly. On a night such as this, I could not have felt happier. Like the fields and trees around us, our hair, too, was filled with crystals, so that by the time we got home it had turned completely white. All the fires had died out long before, so the only source of heat was from the lightbulb in my room. I had never before appreciated before how much warmth it gave off.

Christmas was a magical time on the threshold of the old and new year, and as such it was a precarious time when anything could happen. In the magic world,

concepts of time and space are different to our own. Just as each time of life and hour of the day has its own significance, so does space. It matters greatly in what direction you walk, or whether you turn left or right. Neither Lot's wife nor Orpheus was sufficiently heedful of this, and when they looked back, they paid the consequences. When women collected plants for rituals, they knew that when they carried their magic prize they must be careful not to see anyone nor be seen, nor turn behind them, nor speak nor spit, because by any one of these actions they might dissipate the power of the magic in space and lose their prize.

In village weddings in the Apuseni, the bridegroom must reject two false brides before he can take the true one. First, an old woman confronts him wearing a wedding crown of straw and carrying a posy of nettles and weeds in her hands. She accuses him of seducing her in the forest and making her pregnant, and attempts to climb over the table at which he and his family are sitting. The bridegroom must naturally prevent this, vigorously denying her claims and sending her away. Then a little girl is brought before him, dressed up as a perfect miniature bride. He tells her she is too young to marry him and sends her away with sweets. When the real bride finally appears, he signals his acceptance by giving her a posy of flowers and she gives him a flower in return. Then she climbs over the table to join her new family. Just as in a fairytale, where only the real prince can break through the thorns to awake Sleeping Beauty, it is only the true bride who can climb over the table to cross from one world into another, from maiden into married state. The false brides cannot do this, the one because she is too old and no longer a virgin and the other because she is too young. Time and space conspire against them both.

Left: *A wayside cross in a Maramureş village.*
Following page, left: *Interior of a house. Note the small iron stove. Everyone has a separate summer kitchen to prevent houses becoming too warm in the hot months.*
Following page, right: *Embroidered cloths are used decoratively at home and in church and hung round icons.*

To cross any threshold is full of risk, like crossing from one world into another: from birth to baptism, from maidenhood to marriage, from life to death, from the village to outside. Doors, gates and village boundaries were places of especially powerful magic and needed to be protected, and for this reason garlic was hung around doors or windows, and crosses placed at geographical boundaries. Walking the boundaries of a parish has magic as well as social significance, which was why there were efforts to suppress the practice in England after the Reformation. Romania has passed the threshold of a new phase of its history by joining the European Union.

Enormous changes are underway. Yet one hopes that somehow Transylvania, itself on a geographical and historical threshold between East and West, will retain its mystical allure. As I had realised at the dance, even though the rituals that had governed people's lives for so long were no longer always conscious, they existed at a subliminal level. As the poet Lucian Blaga wrote, the soul of a Transylvanian village does not race like a heart beating in a body, but moves slowly as though it were somewhere deep inside the earth.

Bibliography

Achim, Viorel, *Ţiganii în Istoria României* (Bucharest, 1998).

Alexandru, Tiberiu, *Romanian Folk Music*, trans. Constantin Stihi-Boos, trans. rev. A. L. Lloyd (Bucharest, 1980).

Alterescu, Simion (ed.) *Istoria Teatrului în România*, vol. 1 (Bucharest, 1965).

Andreescu, Stefan, *Vlad the Impaler* (Dracula) (Bucharest, 1999).

Bârcă, Ana, *The Wooden Architecture of Maramureş* (with photographs by Dan Dinescu) (Bucharest, 1997).

Baring-Gould, Sabine, *The Book of Werewolves* (London, 1865).

Bartók, Béla, *Letters,* ed. Janos Demeny, trans. Peter Balaban and Istvan Farkas, trans. rev. Elisabeth West and Colin Mason (London, 1971).

Baumann, Hellmut, *Greek Wild Flowers and Plantlore in Ancient Greece*, trans. William T. Stearn and Eldwyth Ruth Stearn (London, 1993).

Bielz, Julius, *The Craft of Saxon Goldsmiths of Transylvania* (Bucharest, 1957).

Bogdan, Ioan, *Vlad Tepeş şi Naraţiunile Germane şi Ruseşti asupra lui* (Bucharest, 1896).

Boia, Lucian, *Romania: Borderland of Europe* (London, 2001).

Boner, Charles, *Transylvania, its Products and its People* (London, 1865).

Brandsch, Hans-Heinz, Heltmann, Heinz, and Lingner, Walter, *Schässburg: Bild einer siebenbürgischen Stadt* (Thaur bei Innsbruck, 1994).

Browning, Robert, *The Pied Piper of Hamelin* (London, 1842).

Campenhausen, Leyon Pierce Balthasar von, Baron, *Travels through Several Provinces of the Russian Empire; with an historical account of the Zaporog Cossacks, and of Bessarabia, Moldavia, Wallachia, and the Crimea* (London, 1808).

Carcopino, Jérôme, 'Les richesses des Daces et le redressement de l'Empire Romain sous Trajan', *Dacia*, vol. 1, 1924, pp. 28–34.

Carpathian Large Carnivore Project Reports available from www.clcp.ro.

Cassius Dio, *Dio's Roman History*, trans. Earnest Cary, 9 vols, Loeb Classical Library (London, 1914–27).

Cioran, Emil, *Schimbarea la faţă a României* (Bucharest, 1999, first published 1936).

Conduratu, Gregor C., *Michael Beheim's Gedicht über den Woiwoden Wlad II Drakul* (Bucharest, 1903).

Constantinescu, Nicolae, *Romanian Folk Culture* (Bucharest, 1999).

Daicovici, Constantin, 'Fouilles et recherches a Sarmizegetusa: I-er Compte-rendu', *Dacia*, vol. 1, 1924, pp. 224–63.

Drace-Francis, Alexander, 'The Romanians', in Christopher John Murray (ed.) *Encyclopedia of the Romantic Era*, 1760–1850, vol. 1 (New York and London, 2004).

Draguţ , Vasile, 'Picturile Murale de la Mediaş, o Importantă Recuperare Pentru Istoria Artei Transilvănene', in *Revista muzeelor si monumentelor istorice, Monumente istorice şi de arta*, vol. 2, 1976, pp. 11–22.

Edmondson, J.C. 'Mining in the later Roman Empire and beyond: continuity or disruption?', *Journal of Roman Studies*, vol. LXXIX, 1989, pp. 84–102.

Edsman, Carl-Martin, 'Bears', in Mircea Eliade (ed.) *The Encyclopedia of Religion*, vol. 2 (New York, 1987), pp. 86–9.

Fabini, Hermann, *Atlas der siebenbürgisch-sächsischen Kirchenburgen und Dorfkirchen* (Sibiu and Heidelberg, 1999).

Florescu, Radu, *In Search of the Pied Piper* (London, 2005).

Florescu, Radu, and McNally, Raymond, *Dracula: Prince of Many Faces* (New York, 1989).

Fonseca, Isobel, *Bury Me Standing, the Gypsies and their Journey* (London, 1995).

Gerard, Emily, 'Transylvanian superstitions', *The Nineteenth Century*, vol. XVIII, July–December 1885, pp. 130–50.

Gerard, Emily, *The Land Beyond the Forest* (London, 1888).

Gérando, Auguste de, *Transylvanie* (Paris, 1845).

Giurgiu, Emil, *Sighişoara* (Bucharest, 1982).

Goldsworthy, Vesna, *Inventing Ruritania: The Imperialism of the Imagination* (New Haven and London, 1998).

Herodotus, *The Histories*, trans. Robin Waterfield, intro. Carolyn Dewald (Oxford, 1998).

Hitchens, Keith, *A Nation Discovered: Romanian Intellectuals in Transylvania and the Idea of Nation 1700–1848* (Bucharest, 1999).

How, W.W., and Wells, J.A., *Commentary on Herodotus* (Oxford, 1928).
Ionescu, Stefano, *Antique Ottoman Rugs in Transylvania* (Rome, 2005).
Klaniczay, Gabor, 'The decline of witches and the rise of vampires under the eighteenth-century Habsburg monarchy', in Brian P. Levack (ed.) *Witch-Hunting in Continental Europe* (New York and London, 1992), pp. 262–86.
Kligman, Gail, *The Wedding of the Dead* (Berkeley, 1988).
Kyle, Elizabeth, *The Mirrors of Versailles* (London, 1939).
Magris, Claudio, *Danube*, trans. Patrick Creagh (London, 2001).
Mercati, Giovanni, *Opere Minori*, vol. IV (Vatican, 1937).
Millar, Fergus, 'Condemnation to hard labour in the Roman Empire, from the Julio-Claudians to Constantine', *Papers of the British School at Rome*, vol. LII, 1984, pp. 124–47.
Miller, Elizabeth, Dracula: *Sense and Nonsense* (Westcliff-on-Sea, 2000).
Oişteanu, Andrei, *Cosmos vs Chaos: Myth and Magic in Romanian Traditional Culture* (Bucharest, 1999).
Ozanne, James William, *Three Years in Roumania* (London, 1878).
Pavelescu, Gheorghe, *Magia la Români* (Bucharest, 1998).
Petre, Cipriana, and Tanasescu, Antoaneta (eds) *Ten Steps Closer to Romania* (Bucharest, 1999).
Petrescu, Monica, 'The long shadow of Dracula', *The Sunday Telegraph*, 6 February 2005.
Picard, Liza, *Elizabeth's London* (London, 2003).
Rezzori, Gregor von, *Memoirs of an Anti-Semite* (London, 1983).
Stoker, Bram, *Dracula* (London, 1897).
Strabo, *The Geography of Strabo*, trans. Horace Leonard Jones, 8 vols, Loeb Classical Library (London, 1917–32).
Summers, David, 'Living legends in Romania', *Folklore*, vol. 83, Winter 1972, pp. 321–8.
Treptow, Kurt (ed.) Dracula: *Essays on the Life and Times of Vlad Tepeş* (New York, 1991).
Tröster, Johannes, *Das alt- und neu-teutsche Dacia: das ist: Neue Beschreibung des Landes Siebenbürgen*, intro. Ernst Wagner (Cologne, 1981, first published 1666).
Verstegan, Richard, *Restitution of Decayed Intelligence in Antiquities, Concerning the Most Noble and Renowned English Nation by the Study and Travel of RV* (English edition 1673, first published Antwerp 1605).
Vulcănescu, Romulus, *Măştile populare* (Bucharest, 1970).
Ware, Timothy, *The Orthodox Church* (London, 1963).
Wiesel, Elie, *Night*, trans. Stella Rodway (London, 1960).
Wilkinson, William, *An Account of the Principalities of Wallachia and Moldavia with Various Political Observations Relating to Them by William Wilkinson, Esq Late British Consul Resident at Bukorest* (London, 1820).

Acknowledgements

I would like to thank especially Dan Dinescu for his magnificent photographs and for his patience, and all who consented to be photographed. Many thanks to my mother who has always supported my ventures; my father, companion on several visits to Romania, whose gentle questions and quiet wisdom have heightened my understanding and enthusiasm, and my siblings Meg, Rupert and Ben who have tolerated me. A big thank you also to Alex Drace-Francis and my father for reading the manuscript and making many useful comments and corrections. And to the following who in various ways have encouraged, offered advice, help, hospitality and information: Clare Alexander, Andrew Allen, Ana Barca, Andreea Bell, Dirk Bennett, Imre Bhanga, William Blacker, Andrei Blumer, Serban Cantacuzino, Gabriella Cardozzo, Jane Chisolm, William Clutterbuck, Nigel Corrie, Julian and Harriet Cotterell, Cristian Ciubotarescu, Caroline Dawnay, Hermann Fabini, Ion and Lizzie Florescu, Moritz Fried, Ruth Gadjowska, John Goodall, Nikki Gordon Bowe, Friedrich Gunesch, James Hart Dyke, Nancy Marten, Ion Minoiu, Iulia and Avram Negrea, Michi Nestor, John Nicoll, Richard Proctor, Elisabeth Ratiu, Mihai Rasnoveanu, Georgina Rhodes, Tim Richardson, Libby Temperley-Shell, Ileana Troiano, Tudor Voichita, Charles Walker, John Wyllie.

Index

***Right:** Tastes in interior decoration are changing.*

Cas fovia
Carpatus berg
Nö sen
Vacia
Agria
Presburg
Vngern
Varadinū
Gran
Ofen
Stulwyssenb.
Colocia
Segedinū